STEVEN & LINDA

D0823741

HEART-CRY FOR REVIVAL

Oh, that you would tear the heavens open
and come down—
at your Presence the mountains
would melt.
ISAIAH 64:1

Heart-Cry for Revival

by Stephen F. Olford

EMI BOOKS
MEMPHIS, TENNESSEE

Heart-Cry for Revival—Published
©1962, 1969, 1980

©1987 by Dr. Stephen F. Olford
Heart-Cry for Revival

All rights reserved.
No part of this book may be reproduced
without written permission from
EMI Books
P.O. Box 757800
Memphis, Tennessee 38175-7800

Library of Congress Catalog Card Number 80-52053
ISBN 0 87788-335-1
Printed in the United States of America

DEDICATED TO
*ALL THOSE WHO SHARE WITH ME A
HEART-CRY FOR REVIVAL*

CONTENTS

FOREWARD

As long as men seek God's help in their soul-saving witness to a lost world, this noble volume by Stephen F. Olford entitled *Heart-Cry for Revival* ought to live and be reprinted from generation to generation.

Rather than summarize the message of the chapters, let them speak for themselves with all their moving, heart-warming power to the reader as he prayerfully follows each page. Let it be for me to say that no man on earth is more qualified to write the volume than this gifted pastor and expositor. His background as a child of missionary parents, his successful evangelistic witness in England, and the marvelous success by which God has crowned his efforts in the United States of America and overseas all conspire to give depth and color and moving pertinency to his sermons. There is no preacher alive but who ought to read the book.

It is my humble prayer that God will bless this call to revival to a thousand souls who, in turn, will proclaim its glorious appeal to ten thousand other souls. This would be real revival if such a circle of influence could start with any-one, anywhere and reach out to the ends of the earth and to the shores of eternity. God bless reader and publisher alike as this book is sent forth to oversow in God's grace what Satan has done to ruin and wreck humanity. We need a revival of the saving power of Christ in pulpit and in pew. These expository messages will help bring it about.

W. A. Criswell
Pastor, First Baptist Church
Dallas

Pulsating with prophetic challenge for the individual heart is this clear-cut declaration of the crucial need today for vital Christian reawakening and rededication.

Revival is essential, asserts Stephen F. Olford, to restrain the righteous anger of God...to restore conscious awareness of God...to reestablish the glorious activity of God. The requisites of such faith renewal find distinct definition in these messages through analysis of revival's "Who," "Why," "When" and "Way."

Articulate and firmly rooted in Scriptural precept and promise, this book spells out a compelling dictum of God's sovereign act of restoration—the true capacity of faith that is energized, stabilized and vitalized by Word and Spirit.

Alan Redpath
Former Pastor
Moody Memorial Church
Chicago, Illinois

ACKNOWLEDGMENTS

All Bible references are quoted from the King James Version or the
Revised Standard Version unless otherwise noted. Scripture verses from the
Revised Standard Version of the Bible copyrighted 1946, 1952,
© 1971, 1973. Used by permission.

Acknowledgment is given for:
Permission to quote from an article by the Reverend Duncan Campbell which
appeared in *The Christian Herald,* January 10, 1953.
Permission to use portions of an open letter written by Dr. Frederick A. Tatford
and published in the *Harvester* magazine.
Part of an editorial by Dr. A. W. Tozer for *The Alliance Witness,*
January 25, 1956, by permission.
Quotation, "General Booth's Forecast," adapted from *The Witness,* November
1973, pp. 423-424. Used by permission.
Decision for permission to reprint portions of the article, "Four Great Crises,"
by Billy Graham, © 1957 The Billy Graham Evangelistic Association.
Excerpts from "The Power of Revival: A Study of the Effects of the Wesleyan
Revival," by M. O. Owens, Jr., *The Sword and the Trowel,* February 1970.
Permission to reprint the words of "Come, Holy Spirit"
by John Peterson, © 1971 by Singspiration, Inc. All rights reserved.
Used by permission.
Story on revival from *3000 Illustrations for Christian Service,* Walter B. Knight,
Wm. B. Eerdmans Publishing Co. 1952, p. 566. Used by permission.
Permission to quote article by Dr. F. William Chapman, "The Greatest Sin in
America," as reprinted in *Pulpit Helps,* November 1979.
Published by AMG International, Chattanooga, TN.
Quotation by Sidlow Baxter from *The Herald of His Coming,* Vol. 20,
No. 4 for April 1961.
Lines from a hymn by R. Hudson Pope, quoted by permission from
C.S.S.M. Choruses No. 2.
Excerpt from the article, "When the Wind Comes," *The Prairie Overcomer,*
January 1980, p. 25. Reprinted by permission from *Canadian Weekend,*
October 27, 1979.
Quotation from R.V.G. Tasker, *The General Epistle of James* (Tyndale
New Testament Commentaries), published by Tyndale Press
and Wm. B. Eerdmans Publishing Co., pp. 122-123.
Quotation from the book, *Joseph W. Kemp* by Winnie Kemp, Marshall,
Morgan & Scott, Ltd., 1936. Used by permission.
Interview with Festo Kivengere, "The Revival That Was and Is," © 1976
by *Christianity Today.* Used by permission.

AUTHOR'S NOTE

The following expository sermons were first preached at Calvary Baptist Church in New York City. The one message they spell out is that of a Heart-Cry for Revival. This explains why prayer is the recurring theme throughout these chapters. Whatever aspect of revival we survey, the focus of our attention irresistibly returns to the centrality of prayer. The study of God's Word, the stirrings of the Holy Spirit and the desperate need of the church today are the means that God uses to make us long for revival. This is how these messages came to be born. They make no claim to scholarship or literary excellence. As a matter of fact, the sermons, in the main, are typescripts from tape recordings of my preaching. This will account for their sermonic style and personalized application.

I am deeply indebted to Dr. W.A. Criswell for graciously consenting to write the Forward, and to my friend of many years, Dr. Alan Redpath, for recommending the book. I must also express my gratitude to my secretary, Miss Victoria Kuhl, for typing the manuscript.

It is my sincere prayer that the burden which God has given me for a spiritual awakening in our day may become the Heart-Cry for Revival of all who read these pages.

Stephen F. Olford
President of EMI
Memphis, Tennessee

For my readers to understand the burden of this book, I feel that they should be acquainted with the frame of reference from which I write. Without a definition of terms and an explanation of aims, I might well be misunderstood. So by way of introduction, I want to state briefly what I consider to be the nature of, the need for, and the nearness of revival.

The Nature of Revival

The term "revival" is one which is grossly misunderstood. In many quarters today it is employed to describe evangelistic meetings. Now, while the salvation of sinners and the restoration of backsliders are both by-products of revival, these spiritual experiences cannot be said to define revival.

In seeking to find an answer to the question, "What is revival?" I take the liberty of quoting freely from several authorities who have written on the subject. William B. Sprague says:

> Wherever you see religion rising up from a state of comparative depression to a tone of increased vigor and strength; wherever you see professing Christians becoming more faithful to their obligations, and behold the strength of the Church increased by fresh accessions of piety from the world; there is a state of things which you need not hesitate to denominate a revival of religion.

Charles G. Finney defined revival as "nothing else than a new beginning of obedience to God. Just as in the case of a converted sinner, the first step is a deep repentance, a breaking down of heart, a getting down into the dust before God, with deep humility, and a forsaking of sin."

Joseph W. Kemp, in a presidential address to the Baptist Union of New Zealand, declared:

Revival, strictly speaking, means the reanimating of that which is already living but in a state of declension. It has to do principally with the Church as a whole and Christians as individuals. Evangelism, in our usage of the word, as well as in its derivative sense, refers primarily to the proclamation of the gospel to the unsaved. To make evangelism a synonym of revivalism is untrue to the teaching of the New Testament. The Church is responsible for evangelism and not for revival. We are summoned to evangelism; for revival we are cast upon the sovereign grace of God.

G. J. Morgan put it this way:

It is reviving humanity, strictly speaking, to the sense of God—through the indwelling of the Holy Spirit—to reanimate the life of the believer, not to the unregenerate, as they are "dead in trespasses and sins." There can be no reviving, as there was no life to revive. But whenever Christians are revived, there will always be the conversion of men. It has a twofold meaning, implying the revival of spiritual life and vigor among Christians and the conversion of sinners. It is God manifesting Himself through human life, His redeeming power bursting forth in fruits of righteousness and holiness, in the constitution of His Church, the reproduction of spiritual life, a fresh incarnation of the gladness, the rapture of the gospel of the Galilean fields, of the anguished cry of Pentecost rising into a doxology of redeeming love.

Arthur Wallis, in his book entitled *In the Day of Thy Power*, writes:

The meaning of any word is determined by its usage. For a definition of revival we must therefore appeal to the people of God of bygone years, who have used the word with consistency of meaning down the centuries, until it came to be used in a lesser and more limited sense in modern times. Numerous writings on the subject that have been preserved to us will confirm that revival is divine intervention in the normal course of spiritual things. It is God revealing Himself to man in awful holiness and irresistible power. It is such a manifest working of God that human personalities are overshadowed, and human programs abandoned. It is man retiring into the background because God has taken the field. It is the Lord making bare His holy arm, and working in extraordinary power on saint and sinner.

J. Edwin Orr, who has written so extensively on revival, and whose notable work on the *Second Evangelical Awakening in Britain* should be read by all, sums up our theme in this fashion: "The best definition of revival is the phrase, 'Times of refreshing . . . from the presence of the Lord.' "

Geoffrey R. King in a booklet entitled *Rend the Heavens*, summarizes the concept of revival in these words: "Revival is a sovereign act of God upon the Church whereby He intervenes to lift the situation completely out of human hands and works in extraordinary power."

We gather, then, that revival is that strange and sovereign work of God in which He visits His own people, restoring, reanimating and releasing them into the fullness of His blessing. Such a divine intervention will issue in evangelism though, in the first instance, it is a work of God in the *church* and among individual *believers*. Once we understand the nature of heaven-sent revival we shall be able to think, pray and speak intelligently of such "times of refreshing . . . from the presence of the Lord" (Acts 3:19).

The Need for Revival

There has never been a time in the history of the church when God's people have not had a heart-cry for revival. Even in the midst of appalling moral darkness and spiritual declension there have always been those whose heart-cry has been:

Oh, that you would tear the heavens open
and come down
—at your Presence the mountains would melt,
as fire sets brushwood alight,
as fire causes water to boil—
to make known your name to your enemies,
and make the nations tremble at your Presence,
working unexpected miracles
such as no one has ever heard of before.
(Isaiah 64:1-3) *The Jerusalem Bible*

Speaking for our time, however, I see absolutely no hope outside of a mighty spiritual awakening. This conviction was expressed in unmistakable language sometime ago by outstanding leaders of the Christian Brethren in an open letter published in the *Harvester* magazine. Ponder carefully this appeal:

It is doubtful whether, in this history of the world, there has previously been a period of difficulty so complex in character and so widespread in effect as that through which we are at present passing. A feeling of uncertainty and instability prevails in every circle, and the future seems to hold no sure promise of either peace or prosperity. It was never more true that "upon the earth" there is "distress of nations, with perplexity; ... men's hearts failing them for fear, and for looking after those things which are coming on the earth."

In the midst of change and unreliability, spiritual values alone remain immutable, and there never was a greater need for the reminder of their reality, security, and stability. Yet the Church, which should be proclaiming the glorious news, seems totally inadequate to meet the need. Generally speaking, the lives of Christians do not differ, to any great extent, from the lives of other folk around them. They share the same fears, express the same doubts, feel the same uncertainty, show the same disconcertion. The peace of God and the joy of Christ are little in evidence. The dynamic power of the Holy Spirit is not appropriated.

Unparalleled opportunities present themselves, but there seems a moral and spiritual inadequacy to respond to their challenge.

If there is to be a revival of spiritual life and power, it must originate with the individual believer, and there is a great need for a personal searching of heart and exercise of soul in this matter. The sin, which is spoiling the life of the Christian, must be judged, and put away. The selfishness, which is robbing Christ of the love and devotion which are His due, must be confessed and removed. The ambitions and desires, which are hindering the work of God, must be uprooted and thrown on the refuse heap. A renewal of blessing is dependent upon the restoration of communion and the reconsecration of heart and life.

Many of God's people are longing for a reawakening of the Church and for a revival of the work of God, and not a few are praying that the very difficult conditions of the present day may lead to a reassessment of values and a fresh stirring of love for the Lord.

A renewal of evangelistic fervor and zeal might even yet result in an amazing harvest of souls, and we appeal to all Christians to unite in daily personal prayer, not only for a solution to the pressing practical problems of the present day, but for a definite spiritual revival.

If I understand the contemporary scene at all, then it closely resembles the days of General William Booth, illustrious founder of the Salvation Army, when he analyzed the chief dangers of the twentieth century. As I review his words, I cannot but be struck by their aptness and accuracy. He enumerates six such dangers:

1. Religion without the Holy Spirit. Religion can be found everywhere, for man is a "religious animal." Even atheists have their religion, whether their emphasis be on things or men. But the tragedy is that this type of religion has invaded the church; so most of our religious centers have become institutional systems that most people distrust. The size of a denomination is no indication of its reality or power. Further, a local church may go through the correct motions and express biblical beliefs, yet lack the presence of the Holy Spirit. No amount of orthodoxy can guarantee that God is in or with the congregation, if it lacks a sense of dependence upon Him for all its needs. It can only become another church like that in Laodicea. Such is religion without the Holy Spirit.

2. Christianity without Christ. That great expositor, W. H. Griffiths Thomas, said that Christianity *is* Christ. Without the Lord Jesus being central Christianity is only bare bones. Its doctrines may be known, and even understood, and yet Christ can be left out. This is what has happened in history. Christianity has departed from the Christ of the Bible. The "liberal" Christ is a strange person; he is not the Christ of the apostles. Men have divested Him of all His unique characteristics, and yet claim that they are presenting Christ. The Jesus we hear about today is not the eternal Son of God whose atoning death and triumphant resurrection make possible the redemption of sinful man.

3. Forgiveness without Repentance. This is the day of preaching easy forgiveness. "God is so kind and loving that of course He must forgive us," we like to think and to say, but such concepts have no place . . . in New Testament teaching. God's love is no syrupy, sentimental thing. It cost all the agony of Calvary. . . . Evangelicals, in their . . . desire to become involved with people on the earth level and to identify themselves with their lives are sometimes in danger of encouraging this "easy forgiveness," forgetting the need to maintain the fullness of the gospel message. We must preach repentance, as did John the Baptist. There is no forgiveness without repentance.

4. Salvation without Regeneration. There cannot be genuine salvation without regeneration. This has been one of the criticisms of mass evangelism, that people have followed others without themselves being moved upon by the Spirit of God. We must, however, beware of laying down rules where Scripture does not. Conviction sometimes comes to people in a far stronger sense *after* they have come to Christ than immediately before. Yet we need to be careful not to press for decisions in those to whom we witness, lest they are brought into a false position for which we, rather than they, are to blame. We must give way always to the Holy Spirit, regarding ourselves merely as His tools, that He may accomplish His purposes through us, even in spite of our failings. Salvation must involve and include regeneration.

5. Politics without God. There was a day when people spoke of the "nonconformist conscience," and leading ministers and men in public life stood firmly for Christian principles in the realm of social and political activity. Alas, this is not the normal course in our day. The Church is often silent where it should be vocal, not only in its service to men and women but also in its proclamation of the Ten Commandments, and the gospel of sin and salvation. Politics can become thoroughly corrupt when God is left out. When Christian men enter into public life, whether locally or nationally, they can do great good, so long as they follow God's call and walk in the light of God's Word.

6. Heaven without Hell. C. S. Lewis was one who stood firmly for the truth of the righteousness of God. He maintained that God was Judge, as well as a loving Father. Yet the normal attitude today is to deny the gravity of sin, and often, the existence of the devil. Sin is explained away; God is all-merciful and will pass over our sins. Universalism is widely held and taught, that all men will ultimately be saved. The reality of hell is ignored. Just as people are prepared at times to talk about God but ignore Jesus Christ, so they are willing enough to talk about heaven but to pass over hell as no more than a myth.

As William Booth saw it, these are the dangers that would

affect the twentieth century—and how right he was! The question arises, then, as to how these trends can be reversed. Very simply, the answer is revival. Yes, we need revival.

The Nearness of Revival
I still remember the spiritual awakening which visited the Hebrides in 1949. God's servant used in this gracious moving of the Holy Spirit was the Rev. Duncan Campbell. In recounting the story of God's dealings with His people, Mr. Campbell stated:

> I personally believe in the sovereignty of God in the affairs of men, but I do not believe in any concept of revival that eliminates man's responsibility. Here were men and women who believed in a covenant-keeping God, who believed that the God to whom they prayed could not fail to fulfill His covenanted engagements; but they also believed that they too had to do something about it. God was the God of Revival, but they were the instruments, the agents through which revival was possible.

The real issue, then, is how to get ready for revival in the day of His power. To help us in our thinking and praying, and also to condition our hearts for the chapters that follow, I want to quote Dr. A. W. Tozer, in his own right a prophet of righteousness and revival:

1. Get thoroughly dissatisfied with yourself. Complacency is the deadly enemy of spiritual progress. The contented soul is the stagnant soul. When speaking of earthly goods Paul could say, "I have learned . . . to be content"; but when referring to his spiritual life he testified, "I press toward the mark." So stir up the gift of God that is in thee.

2. Set your face like a flint toward a sweeping transformation of your life. Timid experimenters are tagged for failure before they start. We must throw our whole soul into our desire for God. "The kingdom of heaven suffereth violence, and the violent take it by force."

3. Put yourself in the way of the blessing. It is a mistake to look for grace to visit us as a kind of benign magic, or to expect God's help to come as a windfall apart from conditions known and met. There are plainly marked paths which lead straight to the green pastures; let us walk in them. To desire revival, for instance, and at the same time to neglect prayer and devotion is to wish one way and walk another.

4. Do a thorough job of repenting. Do not hurry to get it over with. Hasty repentance means a shallow spiritual experience and lack of certainty in the whole life. Let godly sorrow do her healing work. Until we allow the consciousness of sin to wound us we will never develop a fear of evil. It is our wretched habit of tolerating sin that keeps us in our half-dead condition.

5. Make restitution wherever possible. If you owe a debt, pay it, or at least have a frank understanding with your creditor about your intentions to pay, so your honesty will be above question. If you have quarreled with anyone, go as far as you can in an effort to achieve reconciliation. As fully as possible make the crooked things straight.

6. Bring your life into accord with the Sermon on the Mount and such other New Testament Scriptures as are designed to instruct us in the way of righteousness. An honest man with an open Bible and a pad and pencil is sure to find out what is wrong with him very quickly. I recommend that the self-examination be made on our knees, rising to obey God's commandments as they are revealed to us from the Word. There is nothing romantic or colorful about this plain downright way of dealing with ourselves, but it gets the work done. Isaac's workmen did not look like heroic figures as they digged in the valley, but they got the wells open, and that was that they had set out to do.

7. Be serious-minded. You can well afford to see fewer comedy shows on TV. Unless you break away from the funny boys, every spiritual impression will continue to be lost to your heart, and that right in your own living room. The people of the world used to go to the movies to escape serious thinking about God and religion. You would not join them there, but you now enjoy spiritual communion with them in your own home. The devil's ideas, moral standards and mental attitudes are being accepted by you without your knowing it. And you wonder why you can make no progress in your Christian life. Your interior climate is not favorable to the growth of spiritual graces. There must be a radical change in your habits or there will not be any permanent improvement in your interior life.

8. Deliberately narrow your interests. The Jack-of-all-trades is the master of none. The Christian life requires that we be specialists. Too many projects use up time and energy without bringing us nearer to God. If you will narrow your interests God will enlarge your heart. "Jesus only" seems to the unconverted man to be the motto of death, but a great company of happy men and women can testify that it became to them a way into a world infinitely wider and richer than anything they had ever known before. Christ is the essence of all wisdom, beauty and virtue. To know Him in growing intimacy is to increase in appreciation of all things good and beautiful. The mansions of the heart will become larger when their doors are thrown open to Christ and closed against the world and sin. Try it.

9. Begin to witness. Find something to do for God and your fellow men. Refuse to rust out. Make yourself available to your pastor and do anything you are asked to do. Do not insist upon a place of leadership. Learn to obey. Take the low place until such time as God sees fit to set you in a higher one. Back your new intentions with your money and your gifts, such as they are.

10. Have faith in God. Begin to expect. Look up toward the throne where your Advocate sits at the right hand of God. All heaven is on your side. God will not disappoint you.

If you will follow these suggestions you will most surely

experience revival in your own heart. And who can tell how far it may spread? God knows how desperately the church needs a spiritual resurrection. And it can only come through the revived individual.

1

Thus Solomon finished the house of the Lord
and the king's house; all that Solomon had planned to do
in the house of the Lord and in his own house
he successfully accomplished.
Then the Lord appeared to Solomon in the night
and said to him: I have heard your prayer,
and have chosen this place for myself as a house
of sacrifice.
When I shut up the heavens so that there is no rain,
or command the locust to devour the land,
or send pestilence among my people,
if my people who are called by my name
humble themselves, and pray and seek my face,
and turn from their wicked ways,
then I will hear from heaven,
and will forgive their sin and heal their land.

II CHRONICLES 7:11-14

The
What
of Revival

Billy Graham says:

> We need a spiritual revival that will put a new moral fiber
> into our society . . . Ever since the end of World War II
> this country, along with the other English-speaking
> countries, has been plunging into moral corruption at a
> rate that is gaining momentum. Honesty and truthful-
> ness have been thrown out of the window. The United
> States of America is on one mad whirl of amusements
> and pleasure and licentiousness and immorality. Juve-
> nile delinquency is mounting so rapidly we can't keep
> pace with the figures. The drug menace, far from de-
> creasing, is increasing, and claiming new young victims
> every day.
> Some of the identical symptoms that were noticed in

Rome during the last days of the Empire are now observed and felt in our society. Divorce rates are increasing. Racial tensions are worse, not better. Inflation is siphoning off the savings of those with lower incomes. Political issues are dividing us. Confidence in government has been shaken. Walk down the streets of our cities and read the names of the latest films on the marquees. Most of the films deal with sex, crime, and abnormal behavior. One can only ask, what is the country coming to?

As things are, we are being softened up for the kill. We will be done for before the Communist troops ever get here. It is time that we come to the foot of the cross. When we come to the cross and receive Christ as Savior, he gives us the capacity to love our neighbor. There is no superior race in God's sight. God does not look on the outward appearance, he looks on the heart. God sees our pride. We will have to come where we can love each other as neighbors and look through the eyes of Jesus at these problems.

One of the biggest dangers to the Western world today, as I see it, is false religion. The cults are flourishing. Now, God says you can have all the religion you want. I'm not even going to watch you, he says. I'm not going to hear your prayers because you don't mean what you say. It doesn't come from the heart. Thousands of people in our churches are serving God with their lips, but their hearts are far from him. They have never had an encounter with Jesus Christ, have never been born again, have never been converted. God is looking for real and genuine repentance.

In effect, Billy Graham is echoing the passage in II Chronicles which states: "If my people who are called by my name humble themselves, and pray and seek my face, and turn from their wicked ways, then I will hear from heaven, and will forgive their sin and heal their land." In essence, this is the divine philosophy of revival. It teaches that revival implies a spiritual declension; it also teaches that revival involves spiritual awakening. It matters not how dark and depressing a spiritual situation may appear to be; if God's people, who are called by His name will humble themselves, and pray and seek His face, and forsake their sins, God will hear from heaven, forgive their sins and heal their land. In other words, this verse gives us the "what" of a heaven-sent revival. Observe, first of all:

The Basis of Revival

"If my people who are called by my name." Revival is that strange and sovereign work of God in which He visits His own people—restoring, reanimating and releasing them into the fullness of His blessing. Such a divine intervention will issue in evangelism, though, in the first instance, it is a work of God in the church and among individual believers. This is made clear from the words of our text in which God is addressing His *own* people; and while the original message was to the nation of Israel we must not hesitate to apply it to ourselves. The New Testament reminds us that "whatever was written in former days was written for our instruction, that by steadfastness and by the encouragement of the scriptures we might have hope" (Romans 15:4).

It is plain, then, that if revival is to visit the church *there must be a basic relationship of life.* In our English Bible the word "revive" is almost exclusively an Old Testament term. It essentially means "to quicken, recover, or restore," and is always used with reference to God's covenant people. So the Psalmist prays: "Wilt thou not revive us again, that *thy people* may rejoice in thee?" (Psalm 85:6). So when we speak of revival we must not think of the sinner so much as the saint. The sinner needs regenerating; he is "dead through . . . trespasses and sins" (Ephesians 2:1). Nothing but the new birth can bring about a relationship to God. On the other hand, the saint needs reviving. He has life in Christ but he needs life more abundantly. This is why the Lord Jesus said,

"I came that they may have life, and have it abundantly" (John 10:10).

All across our country today we have men and women who claim to be born again. They have life but their relationship with God is flat and meager, not abundant. This is why we need revival. Only when Christians know what it is to be filled with the Holy Spirit will the nation feel the impact of quality Christianity. The Spirit-filled life is not an optional lifestyle, it is a divine obligation. When God says, "Be filled with the Spirit" (Ephesians 5:18), He is not offering a promise, He is issuing a command. Not to obey that command is disobedience, and disobedience is sin. The Bible says, "Whoever knows what is right to do and fails to do it, for him it is sin" (James 4:17). Judged by this standard, how many Christians today are living in sin? This is why the basis of revival is a relationship of life. Only those who have life can have life more abundantly. God says, "If my people ... turn from their wicked ways, then I will hear from heaven, and will forgive their sin and heal their land."

Notice further that if revival is to visit the church *there must be a basic responsibility of love*—"If my people who are called by *my name*." The emphasis, in the Hebrew, is on those who own, or profess, God's name. In the language of the church, such people are Christians; they bear the name of Christ.

The term "Christian" is used three times in the New Testament and each occurrence helps us to understand the responsibility God's people have in bearing the precious name of Christ. When the Apostle Paul confronted Agrippa with the words, "Believest thou the prophets? I know that thou believest," the king replied, "Almost thou persuadest me to be a Christian" (Acts 26:27-28). He understood that being a Christian presupposes a belief in Christ as God's Messiah and the Savior of men. And this is true for you and me today. No one can be a Christian without the exercise of saving faith.

Then we are told that the disciples were called Christians

first in Antioch (Acts 11:26). The name was given to them in contempt because they belonged to Christ. Everybody in Antioch was aware that Christ was alive, and huge crowds were turning to the Lord Jesus as Savior and Master. The impact of their Christian witness was so extraordinary that Barnabas was sent to investigate what was going on. "When he came and saw the grace of God, he was glad; and he exhorted them all to remain faithful to the Lord with steadfast purpose" (Acts 11:23).

The other reference is in I Peter 4:16, where the apostle writes, "If one suffers as a Christian, let him not be ashamed, but under that name let him glorify God." Whether we like to admit it or not, we live in a Christ-rejecting world, and everyone who takes a Christian stand is bound to face opposition and persecution. The Lord promised this very thing. He said, "In the world you have tribulation; but be of good cheer, I have overcome the world" (John 16:33).

And as the days darken and the coming of the Lord draws nearer, we are going to face more and more trouble. Even in this kind of a situation God is willing and waiting to revive His church, but He must have men and women who have a basic relationship of love. He must have people who believe in Christ, belong to Christ, and behave like Christ, and the unmistakable mark of Christian behavior is LOVE—love to God and love to man. It is with this in mind that God says to us, "If my people who are called by my name humble themselves, and pray and seek my face, and turn from their wicked ways, then I will hear from heaven, and will forgive their sin and heal their land."

This, then, is the basis of revival.

But our text takes us further and underscores for us:

The Burden of Revival

"If my people who are called by my name humble themselves, and pray and seek my face, and turn from their wicked ways." The burden of revival can be summed up in one word: prayer. As Dr. Louis L. King has pointed out,

"The Bible and the record of history reveal that there has never been such a thing as a prayerless revival." And Leonard Ravenhill in his book, *Sodom Had No Bible*, writes: "The Church is dying on its feet because it is not living on its knees."

The fact of the matter is that we want the blessing of revival but we are not prepared to assume the burden of revival. And yet God says, "If my people who are called by my name humble themselves, and pray and seek my face, and turn from their wicked ways, then I will hear from heaven, and will forgive their sin and heal their land."

This matter of prayer is so important that the Spirit of God clearly defines this burden in terms of *brokenness in prayer*—"If my people...*humble* themselves." The root meaning of the word is "to bend the knee." "Thus was Midian *subdued* [under Gideon]... so that they lifted up their heads no more" (Judges 8:28). The picture is one of brokenness. The Bible reminds us that "God opposes the proud, but gives grace to the humble" (James 4:6). This is both a solemn as well as a satisfying statement. For God to resist a man, a church, or a nation, is a terrible thing. The writer to the Hebrews warns us that "it is a fearful thing to fall into the hands of the living God" (Hebrews 10:31). But to humble ourselves under the mighty hand of God is to be exalted in due time (I Peter 5:6). Until we know brokenness in prayer we shall never know blessing in prayer.

How graphically this is exemplified in the parable of the Pharisee and the publican (Luke 18:9-14)—"The Pharisee stood and prayed thus with himself, 'God, I thank thee that I am not like other men, extortioners, unjust, adulterers, or even like this tax collector. I fast twice a week, I give tithes of all that I get.' " Five times over the Pharisee uses the personal pronoun "I." He was proud and arrogant, and as a consequence his prayer never reached heaven. By way of contrast, however, the publican, "standing far off, would not even lift up his eyes to heaven, but beat his breast, saying, 'God, be merciful to me a sinner!' " And commenting on this man's brokenness, Jesus declared, "This man went down to his house justified rather than the other; for every one who exalts himself will be humbled, but he who humbles himself will be exalted."

Are we prepared to be broken in order to be blessed? This can only happen as we contemplate the majesty, glory and purity of God, and then see our own wretchedness, as did Moses, Job, Isaiah, Peter and Paul. God must bring us to the place where we cry, "Wretched man that I am! Who will deliver me from this body of death?" (Romans 7:24). Or in the words of Paul Rader:

> *Bring us low in prayer before Thee,*
> *And with faith our souls inspire,*
> *Till we claim, by faith, the promise*
> *Of the Holy Ghost and fire.*

Selflessness in prayer—"If my people ... *pray*." Of the twelve Hebrew words employed to express this single verb "to pray," the one used here means "to judge self habitually" (Robert Young). Our major problem in prayer is the selfishness of our desires and designs. Only the Holy Spirit can put to death selfishness in prayer and substitute selflessness in prayer. Paul makes this clear when he affirms that

> the Spirit helps us in our weakness; for we do not know how to pray as we ought, but the Spirit himself intercedes for us with sighs too deep for words. And he who searches the hearts of men knows what is the mind of the Spirit, because the Spirit intercedes for the saints according to the will of God (Romans 8:26, 27).

Without doubt, this practice of selflessness in prayer is one of the hardest disciplines to achieve. Selfishness is so much part of our nature. Before we know it, we may even find ourselves praying for revival in order to acquire the fame of a Jonathan Edwards or a Charles Finney!

Has it ever occurred to you that sin started in heaven?

When Lucifer, son of the morning, aspired to take the throne of the universe he fell like lightning from heaven. The same sin of self-seeking ruined the Garden of Eden; and it can ruin your life and mine. And believe it or not, that can even happen while we kneel in prayer. This is why it is so important to pray in the Holy Spirit, because one of the ministries of the Spirit is to put to death the manifestations of our self-life. Paul says, "If [we] live according to the flesh [we] will die, but if by the Spirit [we] put to death the deeds of the body [we] will live" (Romans 8:13). Let us daily learn how to accept the sentence of the cross upon our self life, through the power of the Spirit. Only then shall we know how to prevail in prayer.

Earnestness in prayer —"If my people ... *seek* my face." To seek God's face denotes earnestness in prayer. To illustrate this, Jesus told the story of the friend who went to a neighbor's house at midnight to borrow bread for a hungry traveler. With dramatic emphasis, the Master described the persistence with which the night caller sought the face of his friend until his request was fulfilled. Then Jesus added, "Ask, and it will be given you; seek, and you will find; knock, and it will be opened to you" (Luke 11:9).

The Word of God reminds us that "it is time to seek the Lord" (Hosea 10:12). In other words, we must avoid the things and people that divert us from deliberately seeking the face of God in these desperate days in which we live. It is true that we may be misunderstood, even misrepresented, but this is part of the price we have to pay for earnestness in prayer.

When Peter was in prison and for a time the voice of the gospel was silenced, we read that the early church prayed "without ceasing" for his release (Acts 12:5). This must have involved the denial of food and sleep, and even business, in order to prevail with God. Let us remember that earnestness means seriousness in prayer. When Jacob cried, "I will not let you go, unless you bless me" (Genesis 32:26), he was in earnest, and God rewarded him with blessing.

Holiness in prayer—"If my people . . . *turn from their wicked ways.*" Here, of course, we reach the climax of revival praying. The burden that God would lay upon us is not simply brokenness, selflessness, and earnestness, but *holiness*. James reminds us that "the prayer of a righteous man has great power in its effects" (James 5:16). And Paul exhorts us that "men [should] pray every where, lifting up holy hands, without wrath and doubting" (I Timothy 2:8). And the Psalmist asks, "Who shall ascend the hill of the Lord? and who shall stand in his holy place?" and then gives the answer, "He who has clean hands and a pure heart" (Psalm 24:3, 4). To have defilement on our hands, dissension in our spirits, and doubt in our hearts is to cancel out all our effectiveness in prayer.

Turning from our wicked ways, very often, involves the public confession of our sins. In the Welsh Revival (1904-1905), when more than 100,000 people were converted in the space of five months, Evan Roberts emphasized this matter of public confession of sin. His four points were:

1. The past must be made clear by confession of every known sin to God, and every known wrong to man.
2. Every doubtful thing in the believer's life must be put away.
3. Prompt and implicit obedience must be rendered to the Spirit of God.
4. Public confession of Christ must be made within and without the church.

Reporting on this revival, Dr. G. Campbell Morgan points out that the movement was characterized by the most remarkable confessions of sin—confessions that were costly.

In the 1932 Shantung Revival in China, prisoners would not confess their sins, even though they were tortured unmercifully. But when they came under the power of that revival they admitted their wrongdoings immediately. What torture could not do, the Spirit of God accomplished.

Only the Holy Spirit can convict "the world of sin, ... righteousness, and ... judgment" (John 16:8). We play at prayer when we come into God's presence with unholy lives. There is more said about holiness in the Bible than on any other subject and yet, tragically, this quality is least apparent in the church today. We must hear God saying afresh to us, "Be holy: for I ... am holy" (Leviticus 19:2); and "without [holiness] ... no man shall see the Lord" (Hebrews 12:14). We have confused biblical Christianity with national culture, and have compromised the laws of God with the lusts of man. We will never see revival until we know what it is to "worship the Lord in the beauty of holiness" (Psalm 29:2).

The Blessing of Revival

"If my people who are called by my name humble themselves, and pray and seek my face, and turn from their wicked ways, then I will hear from heaven, and will forgive their sin and heal their land." God is far more ready to bless than we are to receive. It is His very nature to give and to keep on giving. The Bible reminds us that "the Lord God is a sun and shield; he bestows favor and honor. No good thing does the Lord withhold from those who walk uprightly" (Psalm 84:11). "He who did not spare his own Son but gave him up for us all, will he not also give us all things with him?" (Romans 8:32). "God ... richly furnishes us with everything to enjoy" (I Timothy 6:17).

These and other promises all go to show the warmth of God's heart toward man, and what He is willing and waiting to do for us. The only reason we do not know the fullness of blessing is because we have not fulfilled the conditions. But if we understand the basis and the burden of revival we are promised *God's favor*—"Then will I hear from heaven." We notice that the opposite of revival is a closed heaven. God warns, "When I shut up the heavens ... there is no rain." Nothing can be more ominous than a closed heaven. On the other hand, when God looks on His people with divine favor heaven is opened and refreshing rain begins to fall.

We must remember the clear alternatives: either judgment or revival. Many believe that with the prevailing conditions in the Church and in our country judgment is inevitable. If God had to judge the generation of Noah's day, and later the people of Sodom and Gomorrah, is there any hope for us today? And when God judges He begins with His Church, for Peter reminds us that "the time has come for judgment to begin with the household of God" (I Peter 4:17). On the other hand, when the Lord looks with favor on His people the windows of heaven are opened and blessing is poured forth in such measure that there is not room enough to receive it (Malachi 3:10).

Divine favor is one of the guarantees of genuine revival, which someone has described as "a person or a community saturated with the presence of God—an accurate description, for when God breaks into a life, or a community, there is nothing else that matters, except Jesus, the glory of Jesus, the name of Jesus. Revival is not some emotion or worked up excitement, it is rather an invasion from heaven that brings a conscious awareness of God.

God's Word comes alive. A study of revival shows that every visitation from heaven has brought with it a new interest in God's Word. Great doctrines that were forgotten, or neglected, come to light; justification by faith, the forgiveness of sins, the work of the Spirit, the authority of the Bible, and the hope of the Lord's return, and so on.

God's Church comes alive. Christians cease to be passive and assume their true leadership in the family, the church, and the country. They become the "salt" and the "light" in contemporary society.

God's work comes alive. Evangelism and foreign missions have followed every major revival, ever since the days of Pentecost. All this, and more, are the evidence of divine favor. This is what Habakkuk meant when he cried, "Revive thy work in the midst of the years, in . . . wrath remember mercy" (3:2).

God's Fellowship —"Then I will...*forgive their sin.*" Unforgiven sin is the most serious condition in human experience. For the unregenerate, it means ultimate hell; for the believer, it means barrenness and uselessness here on earth, and shame and loss at the judgment seat of Christ. By the same token, forgiven sin is the ground of true fellowship with God. John reminds us that "if we walk in the light, as he is in the light, we have fellowship with one another, and the blood of Jesus his Son cleanses us from all sin" (I John 1:7).

Luke gives us a beautiful description of fellowship in times of revival. After the Holy Spirit had come with renewing wind and refining fire, we read that the disciples "continued steadfastly in the apostles' doctrine and fellowship, and in breaking of bread, and in prayers" (Acts 2:42). No less than seven aspects of this fellowship of revival follow:

There was the fellowship of divine energy—"Many wonders and signs were done by the apostles" (Acts 2:43). When God is at work in a fellowship of believers there is always the evidence of the miraculous—"wonders and signs." Our problem is that we have come to feel that so much of our church life must be explainable in human terms. It may be helpful to become computerized, organized, and publicized but so often we become efficiently dead because we are so suspicious of the miraculous or the supernatural.

There was the fellowship of divine unity—"All who believed were together" (Acts 2:44). Nothing pleases God more than the unity of His people. That is why the Psalmist exclaims, "How good and pleasant it is when brothers dwell in unity!" for there the oil of fragrance, the dew of freshness, and the blessing of fullness are poured out in abundant measure (Psalm 133).

There was the fellowship of divine charity—They "had all things in common; and they sold their possessions and goods and distributed them to all, as any had need" (Acts

2:44, 45). How heartwarming it is when a revival of caring and sharing pervade the people of God! Unfortunately, the opposite is what we usually see today. Materialism, possessiveness and selfishness keep us from true love and fellowship.

There was the fellowship of divine constancy—"Day by day [they attended] the temple together" (Acts 2:46). There was no problem in church attendance, either at the prayer meeting or at the Bible Hour. Only revival can solve the problem of empty churches today.

There was the fellowship of divine radiancy—"They partook of food with glad . . . hearts" (Acts 2:46). That word "glad" describes exuberant joy. One of the fruits of true revival, down through the centuries, has been this quality of joy. We have plenty of superficial or circumstantial happiness and shallow merriment, but so little true joy in the Holy Spirit.

There was the fellowship of divine purity. "They . . . did eat their meat with . . . singleness of heart" (Acts 2:46). The word "singleness" occurs only here in the New Testament. It comes from *apheles* and means "free from rock, stones or grit." It suggests the thought of purity from anything which creates friction in personal or communal life. There was a transparency and openness with God and with one another. Here was a fellowship of believers walking in the light under an unclouded heaven with the ungrieved, unquenched Holy Spirit filling their lives.

There was the fellowship of divine liberty. They were found "praising God and having favor with all the people (they were uninhibited in their witness). And the Lord added to their number day by day those who were being saved" (Acts 2:47). This is what happens when God visits His people in a spiritual awakening.

When the revival of 1858 broke out in the United States it is reported that 50,000 New Yorkers were converted from March to May—a period of three months. During that single year the number of reported conversions throughout the country reached an average of 50,000 a week for a period of two years. There were 10,000 additions to church membership weekly. By actual count, over one million persons were added to the Body of Christ in that brief period. Just to read such figures makes us long for a similar visitation in our time.

God's Fruitfulness—"Then I will...heal their land." As we read the context carefully we see that a closed heaven meant drought, famine and pestilence. No words could better symbolize the problems we now face in our country today, and it is even worse overseas. We must recognize that the material, marital and moral problems of our time are due to spiritual causes. This is why we need revival. There is no situation in contemporary life that cannot be righted by God Almighty—if only He is allowed to work through His revived people. After all, the promise is, "I *will*...heal their land."

God has an answer to material problems. Inflation, energy, unemployment, and a host of other issues, are due to human sin. Call it greed, self-seeking, mismanagement, or whatever, it is human sin. The history of revival is replete with illustrations of how problems like these have been solved by the working of Almighty God.

In the Great Awakening under the Wesleys, problems such as slavery, prison reform, liquor traffic, poor education, were substantially eliminated.

> Wesley fervently believed that Christianity was a religion with social implications. One of his maxims was, "The Gospel of Christ knows of no religion but social, no holiness but social holiness." Thus out of this fire which swept England, Wales and Scotland there came a purifying social reform. Its cleansing power was felt in every direction and in all areas of life. (M. O. Owens, Jr.)

God has an answer to marital problems. Never in our history has there been such a breakdown in married life. In spite of all our seminars, and the flood of literature on topics such as the home and human relationships, we have more people, including preachers, who are being divorced than ever in living memory. Only one thing can solve marital problems and that is revival.

A study of Ephesians, Chapter 5, will establish this beyond dispute. The harmony between husbands and wives, and parents and children, depends upon the fullness and freedom of the Holy Spirit, in marital and family life. It is one thing to have a Pentecost in the church, but quite another matter to experience a Pentecost in the home. In God's economy there is no dichotomy. If we claim to know revival in the church it should also affect our home life. Since the home is the unit of society and the bulwark of national life, we must not rest until God heals the relationships of our homes across our land.

God has an answer to moral problems. M. O. Owens, Jr., in a study of the effects of the Wesleyan Revival in Great Britain, records that

> with the upsurge of the Gospel and the decrease in the consumption of liquor, crime also began to diminish. It became safe to walk the streets of the cities again. Bribery and corruption in business and government lessened. Conversation modulated toward the chaste and decent. The theater became once again the place for art and true entertainment rather than the vulgar and bawdy. The gambling craze almost disappeared, and cruel sports were outlawed.

The effect of the Revival was felt in every area of life. England was once more "merrie England." The full effect is, of course, incalculable. Only eternity can tell of the many lives touched and redeemed. Wesley himself wrote of the results: "Multitudes have been thoroughly convinced of sin, and shortly after, so filled with joy and love that whether they were in the body or out of the body, they could hardly tell; and in the power of this love they have trampled under foot whatever the world accounts either terrible or desirable, having evidenced in their severest trials an invariable and tender goodwill to mankind, and all the fruits of holiness. Now so deep a repentance, so strong a faith, so fervent love, and so unblemished holiness, wrought in so many persons in so short a time, the world has not seen for many ages." No other movement can make a claim comparable to this—to be known as the moral water-shed of Anglo-Saxon history.

When we read accounts like this we have to cry out. "Oh, that you would tear the heavens open and come down—at your Presence the mountains would melt" (Isaiah 64:1); and again: "Wilt thou not revive us again: that thy people may rejoice in thee?" (Psalm 85:6).

I believe that revival for our time is possible. The only question is whether or not we are prepared to take seriously the basis, the burden, and the blessing of revival. God says, "If my people who are called by my name humble themselves, and pray and seek my face, and turn from their wicked ways, then I will hear from heaven, and will forgive their sin and heal their land." Are we ready to take God at His Word, meet His terms, and see Him work in our homes, in our churches, and in our land? Then let us pray with all our hearts:

> *Come, Holy Spirit, dark is the hour—*
> *We need Your filling,*
> *Your love and Your mighty pow'r;*
> *Move now upon us, stir us, we pray,*
> *Come, Holy Spirit, revive the Church today.*
> —John Peterson

2

I will praise thee with my whole heart:
before the gods will I sing praise unto thee.
I will worship toward thy holy temple,
and praise thy name
for thy lovingkindness and for thy truth:
for thou hast magnified thy word above all thy name.
In the day when I cried thou answeredst me,
and strengthenedst me with strength in my soul.
All the kings of the earth shall praise thee, O Lord,
when they hear the words of thy mouth.
Yea, they shall sing in the ways of the Lord:
for great is the glory of the Lord.
Though the Lord be high,
yet hath he respect unto the lowly:
but the proud he knoweth afar off.
Though I walk in the midst of trouble,
thou wilt revive me: thou shalt stretch forth thine hand
against the wrath of mine enemies,
and thy right hand shall save me.
The Lord will perfect that which concerneth me:
thy mercy, O Lord, endureth for ever:
forsake not the works of thine own hands.

PSALM 138 (KJV)

The
Who
of Revival

In a certain town there had been no revival for many years. The church was nearly run out. The people were unconverted. Spiritual desolation reigned. In the town lived an old blacksmith, who stammered so badly that it was painful to hear him speak. At work in his shop he became greatly burdened about the church; his agony became so great that one day he locked the door and spent the afternoon in prayer. After prevailing with God, he obtained the reluctant consent of his pastor to call a church meeting, though with no hope on the preacher's part of any attendance. But the room was more than filled. All present were silent for a time until one sinner broke out in tears and begged, if anyone would pray, to pray for him. Others followed, and it was found that people from every quarter of the town had been under deep conviction from the time the old man was praying in his shop. A powerful revival followed. The stammering man prevailed and, as a prince, had power with God.

The Bible records an occasion when a fainting David prayed like that stammering blacksmith. He sensed his weakness and failure and cried to the Lord and was revived. Later he could testify:

> In the day when I cried thou answeredst me, and strengthenedst me with strength in my soul. . . . Though I walk in the midst of trouble, thou wilt *revive me:* thou shalt stretch forth thine hand against the wrath of mine enemies, and thy right hand shall save me. The Lord will perfect that which concerneth me: thy mercy, O Lord, endureth for ever: forsake not the works of thine own hands (Psalm 138:3, 7, 8).

In these words David personalized his longing for revival. He realized that before he could know the renewing power of God in his life he had to admit his desperate need. Thus the sweet singer of Israel confronts us with "the *who* of revival." He tells us that:

God Revives Those who Confess Spiritual Failure in their Lives

"In the day when I cried thou answeredst me, and strengthenedst me with strength in my soul. . . . Though I walk in the midst of trouble, thou wilt revive me." Revival presupposes failure. It is only those who admit failure and fainting whom God truly revives. In the physical realm, when a man faints and is weak, he needs reviving. In the New Testament we find certain words which are the spiritual expression of a fainting man. The first one is *prayerlessness.* Jesus said, "Men ought always to pray, and not to faint" (Luke 18:1). If a man is not praying, he is fainting. The word "to faint" here is "to cave in" or "to break down." Does that describe your prayer life? Is that why you need revival?

It is my profound conviction that prayerlessness is the out-standing sin in the Church of Jesus Christ today. The least popular and the worst attended gathering so often is the prayer meeting. Since the church is made up of individuals, the question comes back to you and me: What about prayer-lessness in your life, in my life? How we need to cry with David, "Thou wilt revive me."

Dr. F. William Chapman recalls how he heard an evange-list preach at the First Baptist Church of Chickasaw, Ala-bama. His name was Jess "Hell Fire" Henley, from At-lanta, Georgia. He announced that he was going to preach in the Sunday evening service on the subject, "The Greatest Sin in America." That Sunday night the church was packed. Everyone had come to hear of this "great sin" in our beloved nation. Was it to be murder, adultery, rape, alcohol, or some other "big sin" we usually place at the top of the list of wrongdoings? No, a thousand times no! Rather, Jess Henley preached that night on the subject: *Prayerlessness ... The Greatest Sin in America!*

Jess Henley was right. What was true in that yesteryear is much more so today. Seemingly the people of God are doing everything in America today except praying! We can plan programs, promote rallies, raise money, exalt personalities, play softball, swallow goldfish, and many other "good things" with the best of them but we can't get the people of God to attend real prayer meetings.

We have substituted for prayer everything from "soup to nuts" on Wednesday nights in the churches in an at-tempt to get God's people to be faithful. Beloved, I do not care what the "soup to nuts" program you have on Wednesday night is, it is no *substitute for prayer.* For you see ... *there is no substitute for prayer* ... not with our Lord! But, you say, "preacher, the emphasis on *bigness* in our day demands that we do the above things in our churches." Beloved, when will we ever learn how *small* bigness is in God's sight unless it is *spiritual* bigness?

To build a by-pass around the city of prayer is the greatest mistake (sin), that our Lord's churches and people commit today. Yes, it takes valuable time to go through the city of prayer as we travel in this life ... but believe me ... it is well worth it! (Please read James 5:16b).

In the April 6, 1979 issue of *Christianity Today* (p. 52), there is a report of leaders of renewal (revival) ministries from across America. A major concern of the group as they met was the matter (sin) of prayerlessness. They cited recent studies showing that *"the average pastor surveyed prays only three minutes each day!"* Beloved, the *curse of prayerless preachers* is *powerless pulpits* which *produces problem pews* ... Little wonder that our churches are so *spiritually* sick in our day. One thing is sure and certain ... we shall never see *real* revival in America until God's people get serious about their prayer life!

E. M. Bounds, the great prophet of prayer, said: "Every revival of which we have any record has been bathed in prayer."

Beloved, it is bath time.

If prayerlessness is the greatest sin, there is an aspect of this prayerlessness that is of particular concern in heaven. Isaiah records that God "wondered that there was no intercessor [on earth]" (Isaiah 59:16). Indeed, it was because there was no qualified human mediator that God brought salvation at the first advent of Jesus Christ. And while here upon earth He exemplified, as no one else in history, what it means to be an intercessor. A careful study of the high priestly prayer in John 17 makes this abundantly clear. Now in resurrection glory and power our Savior ever lives to make intercession for us. But as He looks down upon the world scene at this point in time, I have a feeling that He wonders again that there are so few intercessors within His church.

Dr. Sidlow Baxter highlights the need for intercessory prayer when he writes:

We need a revival of intercessory prayer among God's own people. We do not pray enough. Besides intensifying their private prayer life, Christians should band themselves into cottage prayer groups to lay hold upon God for revival in our own land and in every land. Our most pressing need at this moment is to ask God to give more mighty prayer to all who can have at heart the speedy evangelization of every unreached soul—prayer that is strong, prevailing, believing, God-moving, hell-defeating, devil-routing, sinner-saving, believer-sanctifying, Christ-exalting, worker-producing and money-finding!—prayer that takes all we are and have, to offer it to God, as it took all that Jesus had, on Calvary, to give us the right to pray.

But where in all the world are we going to get prayer that will do that?—the kind that Daniel offered, which shook the Babylonian Empire from end to end, bringing Almighty God into His rightful preeminence; the kind that Nehemiah offered, which set rulers running after him with men, money, and materials, to help rebuild the walls of ruined Jerusalem. It was God Himself Who inspired the prayer of Nehemiah, the prayer that made Jerusalem a new city. He drove His servant to his knees by the burden of a great concern for ruined Jerusalem. This seems to be the way God works. And will God give this kind of prayer today? Yes, through the Holy Spirit, God can give us the hurricane kind of prayers that make things move when nothing else can make them move.

We must get God's prayer—prayer with extraordinary consequences! Prayers which are merely our own are futile and get us nowhere. The devil fears nothing that man makes—not even his prayers! He only begins to feel alarm when a soul begins to offer before God the prayer that is Spirit-inspired, and which was born in the very heart of God Himself. It is prayer shot through with the very blood and passion of the Son of God, filled with the power and persistence of the Holy Ghost, loaded with a burdening sense of the church's plight, and the world's appalling need, that sets the wheels of Revival in motion!

God save us from trying to turn these wheels by our own efforts! It cannot be done. Let us beg God now for this kind of praying—prayer straight from God, to straighten out every tangle and to meet every need. When we offer His prayer, as put into our spirits, there will be no such thing as unanswered prayer. Every prayer will be as almighty as God because His nature will be in them. The difficulties we face at the present time will vanish, and we shall not speak as if God were bankrupt!

God will then be seen in our lives. His power will flow through us in flood-tides of blessings to others. Miracles will happen in every sphere that we touch. Every need will be met: and the devil will be defeated. May this heaven-born flame be lighted afresh in the hearts of the regenerate throughout the world.

But spiritual fainting also demonstrates *fearfulness.* Remember how the writer to the Hebrews challenges this sin of fearfulness when he writes: "Consider him who endured from sinners such hostility against himself, so that you may not grow weary or fainthearted. In your struggle against sin you have not yet resisted to the point of shedding your blood" (Hebrews 12:3-4). Here "to faint" means "to relax," or "to let out rope." How many Christians are relaxing instead of fighting sin; letting out rope with evil instead of coming to grips with it and slaying it in the name of the Lord. In the Book of Jeremiah God says to us, "Cursed is he who keeps back his sword from bloodshed" (Jeremiah 48:10). Can you honestly say, "As God is my record, I am *not* afraid of holiness; I am *not* fearful of going all the way with God, cost me what it will; I will *not* hesitate for fear of being thought super-spiritual"?

Fainting not only suggests prayerlessness and fearfulness, but also *barrenness*—"Let us not be weary in well doing," says Paul, "for in due season we shall reap, if we faint not" (Galatians 6:9). The apostle points out that to faint or relax is to be barren, to lose the fruitfulness of harvest. "We shall reap, if we faint not." Do you need revival because you are barren in life and service? Then face up to it and be honest in your confession of failure. Pray and mean the words—"Lord, revive me, for I am prayerless, fearful and barren."

God Revives Those who Profess Practical Faith in their Lives

James reminds us that "faith without works is dead" (James 2:20). A working faith is one which believes in the ability of God to do anything in His divine purpose and for His divine glory. In this context we need to have faith in *a God of personal revival*—"Thou wilt revive me." All through the Bible we have instances of the divine/human encounter. When Abraham reached the point in his life when he was prepared to give his all, God said to him, "Because thou hast done this thing . . . in blessing I will bless thee" (Genesis 22:16, 17). Later we read of Jacob who, having been broken in struggle with the heavenly wrestler, cried out, "I will not let thee go, except thou bless me" (Genesis 32:26). Remember, too, the impassioned prayer of Jabez, "Oh that thou wouldest bless me indeed" (I Chronicles 4:10).

So often we dodge the real issue by praying for it in broad, general terms, not recognizing that before God can bless others He wants to bless us personally. Elizabeth Codner sensed this *personal* need when she wrote her hymn, "Even Me." This was in 1860, when revival was taking place in Ulster and Wales, and she longed that the blessing might visit her and spread through England. Weigh the words carefully:

Lord! I hear of showers of blessing
  Thou art scattering full and free—
Showers the thirsty soul refreshing;
  Let some drops now fall on me,
              Even me.

Pass me not, O gracious Father!
  Lost and sinful though I be;
Thou might'st curse me, but the rather
  Let Thy mercy light on me,
              Even me.

Pass me not, O tender Savior!
  Let me love and cling to Thee:
Fain I'm longing for Thy favor;
  When Thou callest, call for me,
              Even me.

Pass me not, O mighty Spirit!
  Thou canst make the blind to see;
Testify of Jesus' merit,
  Speak the word of peace to me,
              Even me.

Have I long in sin been sleeping,
  Long been slighting, grieving Thee?
Has the world my heart been keeping?
  Oh! forgive and rescue me,
              Even me.

Love of God! so pure and changeless;
  Love of Christ! so rich and free;
Grace of God! so strong and boundless,
  Magnify it all in me,
              Even me.

Pass me not, Almighty Spirit!
   Draw this lifeless heart to Thee;
   Impute to me the Savior's merits;
   Blessing others, oh! bless me,
                  Even me.

Then we must have faith in *a God of purposeful revival*—
"Thou *wilt* revive me. . . . The Lord will perfect that which
concerneth me: thy mercy, O Lord, endureth for ever: forsake not the works of thine own hands." God's supreme
purpose for your life and mine is perfection. That thought
is echoed and reinforced in the New Testament. Jesus said:
"Be ye therefore *perfect,* even as your Father which is in
heaven is perfect" (Matthew 5:48).

Paul declares that his object in preaching the gospel is
that he might be able to present "every man *perfect* in Christ
Jesus" (Colossians 1:28). Elsewhere he tells us that "all
scripture is given by inspiration of God, and is profitable
for doctrine, for reproof, for correction, for instruction in
righteousness: That the man of God may be *perfect,* thoroughly furnished unto all good works" (II Timothy
3:16-17). God's purpose in revival is to perfect us in His
blessed Son, by the power of the Holy Spirit.

Our faith must be in a God of personal revival, a God of
purposeful revival and *a God of powerful revival*—"Thou
wilt *revive* me." The word "revive" means "to reanimate."
In the great activities of God we read of His work in the
realms of creation, recreation and then of reanimation.
When He created He brought the first man into existence.
When He recreates He brings the new man into being; but
when there is backsliding He sends revival to reanimate or
revitalize. Have we the faith to believe God for this?

God Revives Those who Express Biblical Foresight in their Lives

"Though I walk in the midst of trouble, thou wilt revive me:
thou shalt stretch forth thine hand against the wrath of

mine enemies, and thy right hand shall save me." Anyone who knows his Bible recognizes that the Christian on earth is going to be confronted with tribulation and opposition. As we shall see in a moment, Jesus promised such times of testing and trial right through to the end of the journey. In the light of this, how important it is for the believer to face life in a state of spiritual revival!

Think for instance of *the tribulation in the world*. Jesus said: "In the world you have tribulation; but be of good cheer, I have overcome the world" (John 16:33). David is saying the same thing when he affirms, "Though I walk in the midst of trouble, thou wilt revive me." The child of God may sometimes be revived *out* of trouble, more frequently revived *in* trouble, and often revived *through* trouble.

When the three youths, who knew the God of triumph, were in the fiery furnace, their persecutor, Nebuchad-nezzar, had to say: "Lo, I see four men loose, walking in the midst of the fire, and they have no hurt; and the form of the fourth is like the Son of God" (Daniel 3:25). Conquest amid the tribulations of life is the hallmark of genuine Christianity. The Christian is a man who acts victoriously and redemptively in stressful situations. He is not bound by trouble or persecution. Because he is walking through the fire *in the company of the Son of God* his movements are free, his being unharmed. He is spiritually alive in the place of death. That is the victory of revival!

Then there is *the opposition of the world*. In His Sermon on the Mount the Savior taught: "Blessed are you when men revile you and persecute you and utter all kinds of evil against you falsely on my account. Rejoice and be glad, for your reward is great in heaven, for so men persecuted the prophets who were before you" (Matthew 5:11-12). And this is virtually what David is telling us in his psalm: "Thou shalt stretch forth thine hand against . . . mine enemies, and thy right hand shall save me."

There was a day in the life of David when he "waxed faint" and would have been slain by one of the sons of the giant, but Abishai came to his aid, smote the Philistine, and saved his king (II Samuel 21:15-17). Tell me, are you waxing faint in the battle against the Philistines? Is the opposition of the world too hot for you? Then ask the Lord to revive your experience of the heavenly Abishai that you might be able to conquer the enemies of your soul. The truly revived Christian can say, and mean, "I am more than conqueror through Him who loved me" (Romans 8:37).

So we have seen the kind of people whom God is prepared to revive. They are the men and women who are ready to confess spiritual failure in their lives, whether of prayerlessness, fearfulness or barrenness; people who are ready to profess practical faith in a God who revives personally, purposefully, and powerfully; people who are ready to express biblical foresight in their lives, fully prepared for tribulation or opposition when it comes. Will you pray, "Revive me," and then open your being to the Spirit of Revival? Do not rest until you have been restored to the fullness of the blessing that God is waiting to pour out in your life!

3

Lord, thou wast favorable to thy land;
thou didst restore the fortunes of Jacob.
Thou didst forgive the iniquity of thy people:
thou didst pardon all their sin.
Thou didst withdraw all thy wrath; thou didst turn
from thy hot anger.
Restore us again, O God of our salvation,
and put away thy indignation toward us!
Wilt thou be angry with us for ever?
Wilt thou prolong thy anger to all generations?
Wilt thou not revive us again, that thy people
may rejoice in thee?
Show us thy steadfast love, O Lord,
and grant us thy salvation.
Let me hear what God the Lord will speak,
for he will speak peace to his people,
to his saints, to those who turn to him in their hearts.
Surely his salvation is at hand for those who fear him,
that glory may dwell in our land.
Steadfast love and faithfulness will meet;
righteousness and peace will kiss each other.
Faithfulness will spring up from the ground,
and righteousness will look down from the sky.
Yes, the Lord will give what is good,
and our land will yield its increase.
Righteousness will go before him,
and make his footsteps a way.

PSALM 85

The
Why
of Revival

Elijah was the famous prophet of the 9th century B.C. who served in the northern kingdom in the reigns of Ahab and his son, Ahaziah. His consuming passion throughout his ministry was the vindication of God's ways among men. His encounter with the prophets of Baal on Mount Carmel is perhaps the best illustration of this fact. The story reads like a thriller.

After three rainless years the Lord had instructed Elijah to present himself before Ahab. On his way to see the king, the prophet met Obadiah, who was over the king's household, and told him to go and inform the king that he had come. When Ahab met Elijah he greeted him as the "troubler of Israel" (I Kings 18:17), but the prophet replied that it was Ahab who had troubled Israel by forsaking the Lord and following after Baal. He further challenged Ahab to bring to Mount Carmel the 450 prophets of Baal and the 400 prophets of Asherah, who were subsidized by Jezebel the queen.

When these prophets assembled, along with many of the people, God's prophet proposed a test to determine who was the true God. The prophets of Baal were to prepare a meat offering, and Elijah was to do the same; the God who answered by fire and consumed the offering would be recognized as the true God. The efforts of the Baal worshipers proved to be ineffectual, and Elijah mocked them as they tried to induce Baal to receive their offering. Finally, the prophet took charge, prepared the altar of the Lord, laid his offering upon it, and then instructed the people to pour four jars of water on it three times, so that the water soaked the prospective offering.

What a dramatic and dazzling moment it was when Elijah looked up to heaven and cried,

> Hear me, O Lord, hear me, that this people may know that thou art the Lord God... Then the fire of the Lord fell, and consumed the burnt sacrifice, and the wood, and the stones, and the dust, and licked up the water that was in the trench. And when all the people saw it, they fell on their faces: and they said, The Lord, he is the God; the Lord, he is the God (I Kings 18:37-39).

As far as Elijah was concerned, that was the *why* of revival. Nothing else mattered so long as the people knew that God was on the throne and active in history, and longing to heal their land. As in the days of Elijah, so it must be in our times. Nothing really matters except the glory of God.

David focuses on this when he asks, "Wilt thou not revive us again, that thy people may rejoice in thee?" He was looking back to a time when God had been favorable to the land and had "brought back the captivity of Jacob." Then he continues, "Thou didst forgive the iniquity of thy people; thou didst pardon all their sin. Thou didst withdraw all thy wrath; thou didst turn from thy hot anger." He is recalling the time when God delivered Israel from captivity, forgave the iniquity of the people and in sovereign grace restrained the fierceness of His anger.

In the verses that follow the psalmist forecasts the possibility of a coming great national revival. Implicit in his words are the divine principles that underlie spiritual revival when God's people are ready to pay the price. In effect, David gives three reasons why God sends revival.

Revival will Restrain the Righteous Anger of God

Restore us again, O God of our salvation, and put away thy indignation toward us! Wilt thou be angry with us for ever? Wilt thou prolong thy anger to all generations? Wilt thou not revive us again, that thy people may rejoice in thee?

It is clear from these words that God must visit His righteous anger against *an unrevived people*. Their state is vividly described to us in three words which significantly punctuate this psalm.

The first of these words is found in verse 2—"the *iniquity* of thy people." Iniquity denotes *wickedness,* and the tragedy is that such wickedness can be found even in the heart of a redeemed man or woman. Every Christian is possessed of two natures—the old and the new. If he is living in the fullness of the Holy Spirit then the new nature will be dominant and the old will be dormant. On the other hand, if he is living in an unrevived state, ruled by his old nature, then this wickedness will find expression in subtle forms of iniquity. How true are the words of Jeremiah the prophet: "The heart is deceitful above all things, and desperately wicked: who can know it?" (Jeremiah 17:9). Iniquity is that evil in our hearts which tries to explain away God's demands upon our lives in order that we may continue to sin.

The Psalmist says, "If I regard iniquity in my heart, the Lord will not hear me" (Psalm 66:18). This means that if I look with approval upon anything which is out of adjustment to the will of God, I erect a barrier between myself and God so that He will not hear me. Surely this explains why so often our prayers are not answered, our lives are not blessed, and our service is not fruitful. We have explained away the divine commands and lowered the standards of God's expectation in our lives. This in turn leads to what the psalmist plainly calls "sin" in verse 2.

The Apostle John tells us in his epistle that "sin is the transgression of the law," or, as the Revised Standard Version puts it, "Sin is lawlessness" (I John 3:4). Wickedness always leads to *lawlessness*, or the arrogant violation of the will of God. Explain away the divine demands and it becomes all too easy to disobey them. How prevalent this is in the church of Jesus Christ today! Think of the sin of non-attendance at church gatherings (Hebrews 10:25), the sin of unreliability in Christian service (I Corinthians 4:2), the sin of unholiness in everyday life (I Thessalonians 4:7). Every thoughtful Christian must be aware of the fact that we are living in a day of "double standards." A "philosophy of persuasion" is being used to introduce thousands of our young people into ways of immorality, unchastity and easy divorce. But the description does not end there. The psalmist goes on to say that wickedness produces lawlessness, and this in turn leads to *carelessness.* We read that God "will speak peace unto his people, and to his saints: but let them not turn again to *folly.*" How often we hear the expression, "I couldn't care less." Wickedness and lawlessness have produced an insensitivity to evil, leading to a cold, calculated carelessness.

When I look into the faces of Christian men and women who laugh and mock when God is speaking to them about their iniquity and sin and folly, I can understand why God's righteous anger is revealed from heaven. God cannot condemn sin in the sinner and condone it in the saint. This is what Peter means when he says, "For the time has come for judgment to begin with the household of God" (I Peter

4:17). We talk about the judgment of an evil world, but we forget that the risen Lord is Judge also of His own church. As He walks among the candlesticks His eyes burn as "a flame of fire" at the sight of iniquity, sin and folly (Revelation 1:13-14).

God has a high standard of holiness for His Church and His people, and we must not forget it. Consider for instance such utterances as:

Thy decrees are very sure; holiness befits thy house, O Lord, for evermore (Psalm 93:5).

It is written, "You shall be holy, for I am holy" (I Peter 1:16).

For God hath not called us unto uncleanness, but unto holiness (I Thessalonians 4:7).

God's anger is revealed not only against an unrevived people, but also against *an unrepentant people*—"Restore us again, O God of our salvation, and put away thy indignation toward us!" It is one thing to be passively unrevived, but it is worse to be actively unrepentant. For too long now we have thought of the message of repentance only in terms of the unregenerate sinner, but we must remember that God calls His own people to repentance. If you have any doubt about this, get down on your knees and read seriously Chapters 2 and 3 of the Book of the Revelation. Speaking to the church, Jesus says:

I will ... remove your lampstand from its place, unless you repent (2:5).

Repent then. If not, I will come to you soon and war ... with the sword of my mouth (2:16).

Remember ... what you received and heard; keep that, and repent (3:3).

Be zealous and repent (3:19).

Yes, revival is needed to restrain the righteous anger of God.

Revival will Restore the Conscious Awareness of God

Wilt thou not revive us again, that thy people may rejoice in thee? Show us thy steadfast love, O Lord, and grant us thy salvation. Let me hear what God the Lord will speak, for he will speak peace to his people, to his saints, to those who turn to him in their hearts.

Somebody has described revival as "a person or a community saturated with the presence of God," and this is an accurate description; for when God breaks into a life or a community, nothing else matters save the person of Jesus, the glory of Jesus, the name of Jesus. Revival is not some emotion or worked-up excitement; it is rather an invasion from heaven which brings to man a conscious awareness of God.

David Brainerd records the beginning of a wonderful movement among the American Indians in 1745. It all started when the community was gripped with an overwhelming sense of God. He writes:

The power of God seemed to descend upon the assembly "like a rushing, mighty wind" and with an astonishing energy bore down on all before it. I stood amazed at the influence that seized the audience almost universally and could compare it to nothing more aptly than the irresistible force of a mighty torrent... Almost all persons of all ages were bowed down with concern together, and scarce one was able to withstand the shock of this surprising operation.

This conscious awareness of God is implied by the psalmist. He speaks of it as *the smiling of His face*—"Wilt thou not revive us again?" More literally this should read, "Wilt thou not return and revive us again?" In Hebrew thinking, the "turning away of God's face" was recognized as a metaphor for His displeasure. On the other hand, when God responded to a repentant and restored people the picture in their minds was that of a smiling deity. This is the significance of the threefold blessing pronounced by the priests upon the children of Israel: "The Lord bless thee and keep thee: The Lord make his face shine upon thee, and be gracious unto thee: The Lord lift up his countenance upon thee, and give thee peace" (Numbers 6:24-26). The psalmist could also pray, "Make thy face ... shine upon thy servant" (Psalm 31:16). When Absalom was in disgrace we are told that he "dwelt two full years in Jerusalem, and saw not the king's face" (II Samuel 14:28).

Oh, that God would show us His face once again in the person of His beloved Son! Surely this is His purpose in revealing Himself initially and continually to the human soul —for "the God who said, 'Let light shine out of darkness' ... has shone in our hearts to give the light of the knowledge of the glory of God in the face of Christ" (II Corinthians 4:6).

Then there is also *the showing of His grace*—"Show us thy steadfast love, O Lord, and grant us thy salvation." The conscious awareness of God in the believer's life is the guarantee of the grace of victory—"For sin will have no dominion over you, since you are not under law but under grace" (Romans 6:14). Living in grace! That is the divine intention for each believing heart, but do we know this divine mercy and delivering grace day by day?

And if we have an awareness of God we will also know *the sounding of His voice*—"Let me hear what God the Lord will speak, for he will speak peace to his people, to his saints, to those who turn to him in their hearts." Every revival in history has been accompanied by a new recognition of the voice of God. The Bible lives and speaks again. Audiences are hushed under the sound of authoritative, Spirit-empowered preaching.

I remember hearing the Rev. Duncan Campbell tell how preacher and listeners were hushed again and again in the presence of God during the Hebrides Revival. It was just as if God had broken into the situation with the words, "Be still, and know that I am God."

Revival, then, will restore the conscious awareness of God among His people.

Revival will Reveal the Gracious Activities of God

Surely his salvation is at hand for those who fear him, that glory may dwell in our land. Steadfast love and faithfulness will meet; righteousness and peace will kiss each other. Faithfulness will spring up from the ground, and righteousness will look down from the sky. Yea, the Lord will give what is good, and our land will yield its increase. Righteousness will go before him, and make his footsteps a way.

Since the fall of man in the Garden of Eden there has never been a moment in time when God has not been active. Jesus indicated this when He said, "My Father is working still, and I am working" (John 5:17). He is active all over the world at this very hour.

At a missionary conference some years ago I was impressed with the distinct note of *victory* by speaker after speaker—in spite of enemy advances in practically every field of the world. When revival comes it is as if a veil is lifted and we see God in a flood-tide of action in areas where before we had seen nothing but darkness and defeat.

In his book, *In the Day of Thy Power,* Arthur Wallis pictorializes this when he writes:

There was once an ancient reservoir in the hills that supplied a village community with water. It was fed by a mountain stream, and the overflow from the reservoir continued down the streambed to the valley below. There was nothing at all remarkable about this stream. It flowed on its quiet way without even disturbing the boulders that lay in its path or the foot-bridges that crossed it at various points. It seldom overflowed its steep banks, or gave the villagers any trouble. One day, however, some large cracks appeared in one of the walls of the old reservoir, and soon afterwards the wall collapsed, and the waters burst forth down the hillside. They rooted up great trees; they carried along boulders like playthings; they destroyed houses and bridges and all that lay in their path. The streambed could not now contain the volume of water, which therefore flowed over the countryside, even inundating distant dwellings. What had before been ignored or taken for granted now became an object of awe and wonder and fear. From far and near people who in the usual way never went near the stream, hastened to see this great sight.

In picture language, this is revival. At the present time God is at work, like that quiet stream of water, but when revival comes the stream becomes a mighty deluge sweeping everything before it.

The activity of God in the world today is twofold. First, there is *His saving activity*—"Surely his salvation is at hand for those who fear him, that glory may dwell in our land." God is saving men and women all over the world, even though it may seem like a trickle in the great riverbed of human need. But if revival were to visit us the tens would become the hundreds, and the hundreds the thousands, and the thousands the millions. You have only to read the story of the great movements of the Spirit over one hundred years ago in Great Britain and the United States to see what God did in a matter of months. Oh, for another such visitation!

Secondly, there is *His sanctifying activity*. This is demonstrated in *personal life*—"Steadfast love and faithfulness will meet; righteousness and peace will kiss each other." What a delightful portrayal of a sanctified life! Those glorious qualities were gathered up in the nature and personality of our Lord Jesus. When He dwells in us in revival fullness all flesh can *see* the glory of God.

Oswald Chambers used to say, "Sanctification is allowing

the perfections of the Lord Jesus to express themselves in human personality." God wants men and women in whom are married steadfast love, faithfulness, righteousness and peace. "For the kingdom of God is not meat and drink; but righteousness, and peace, and joy in the Holy Spirit" (Romans 14:17).

In *social life*—"Faithfulness will spring up from the ground, and righteousness will look down from the sky." No great religious revival has ever taken place without effecting the most outstanding reforms. Indeed, someone has said that the secret connections between revival and the destiny of nations can be shown to have brought about greater revolutions of history than the Gothic invasions.

Dr. F. B. Meyer once observed that "there has never been a great religious revival without social and political reforms." In this regard we might point out that the abolition of slavery followed a revival. The end of child labor resulted from a revival. Indeed, before the Wesleys and Whitefield preached their flaming messages of revival and reform, people in England were working ninety hours a week. But as a direct consequence of this movement of the Spirit, sixty working hours became the standard, and the first trade unions, in all their purity, were organized. Also flowing like many streams from this spiritual revival were the well-known movements like the YMCA, the Salvation Army, missionary societies, and most of our charitable organizations and educational institutions. We could add to this list slum clearance programs, Sunday School work, and a host of other honored and useful reforms in our religious, social and economic life. A well-known historian says that "the whole temper of the English people was changed" as a result of God at work in His people's lives.

In *material life*—"Yea, the Lord will give what is good, and our land will yield its increase." The most prosperous and glorious periods in British and American history are associated directly with revival. Material advancement as well as the health of the people were fruits of those times of refreshing from the presence of the Lord. And so the psalmist concludes with the words: "Righteousness will go before him, and make his footsteps a way." When the Lord our God moves through a land in revival blessing He lays out a pathway for His people to walk in and inevitably the nation follows, for "righteousness exalts a nation: but sin is a reproach to any people" (Proverbs 14:34). Conversely, where there is no vision the people throw off all moral restraint (Proverbs 29:18).

We set out to answer the question, "Why revival?" The answer is simple, but more than that, it is vital. Revival restrains the righteous anger of God, restores the conscious awareness of God, and reveals the gracious activity of God. In the light of these facts we are driven to pray again, "Wilt thou not revive us again, that thy people may rejoice in thee?"

In 1890 James Gilmour of Mongolia wrote to an old college friend:

> You say you want reviving, go direct to Jesus and ask it straight-out. . . . This revived state is not a thing you need to work yourself up into, or need others to help you rise into, or need to come to England to have operated upon you;—Jesus can effect it anywhere and does effect it everywhere whenever a man or woman, or men and women, ask it.

"Ask, and you will receive" (John 16:24).

Are you prepared to ask for revival? Are you prepared to look for revival? Are you prepared in repentance, faith and obedience to meet the divine conditions for revival? If so, pray with the psalmist, "Wilt thou not revive us again?"

4

A prayer of Habakkuk the prophet,
according to Shigionoth.
O Lord, I have heard the report of thee, and thy work,
O Lord, do I fear. In the midst of the years
renew it; in the midst of the years make it known;
in wrath remember mercy.
God came from Teman, and the Holy One
from Mount Paran. His glory covered the heavens,
and the earth was full of his praise.
His brightness was like the light, rays flashed
from his hand; and there he veiled his power.
Before him went pestilence,
and plague followed close behind.

He stood and measured the earth;
he looked and shook the nations;
then the eternal mountains were scattered,
the everlasting hills sank low. His ways were as of old.
I saw the tents of Cushan in affliction;
the curtains of the land of Midian did tremble.
Was thy wrath against the rivers, O Lord?
Was thy anger against the rivers,
or thy indignation against the sea,
when thou didst ride upon thy horses,
upon thy chariot of victory?
Thou didst strip the sheath from thy bow,
and put the arrows to the string.
Thou didst cleave the earth with rivers.
The mountains saw thee, and writhed;
the raging waters swept on;
the deep grave forth its voice, it lifted its hands on high.

The sun and moon stood still in their habitation
at the light of thine arrows as they sped,
at the flash of thy glittering spear.
Thou didst bestride the earth in fury,
thou didst trample the nations in anger.
Thou wentest forth for the salvation of thy people,
for the salvation of thy anointed.
Thou didst crush the head of the wicked,
laying him bare from thigh to neck.
Thou didst pierce with thy shafts the head
of his warriors, who came like a whirlwind to scatter me,
rejoicing as if to devour the poor in secret.
Thou didst trample the sea with thy horses,
the surging of mighty waters.
I hear, and my body trembles, my lips quiver
at the sound; rottenness enters into my bones,
my steps totter beneath me.
I will quietly wait for the day of trouble to come
upon people who invade us.
Though the fig tree does not blossom,
nor fruit be on the vines,
the produce of the olive fail and the fields yield no food,
the flock be cut off from the fold
and there be no herd in the stalls,
yet I will rejoice in the Lord, I will joy in the God
of my salvation. God, the Lord, is my strength;
he makes my feet like hinds' feet,
he makes me tread upon my high places.
To the choirmaster: with stringed instruments.

HABAKKUK 3

The
When
of Revival

Habakkuk appears on the scene unannounced. Who he was, and of what family or tribe he was born we are not told. Neither do we know very much about the time of his ministry. But we gather from the content of his messages that he came later than Ezra and Nehemiah and the prophets Haggai and Zechariah. His name is obscure, though there are scholars who tell us that it denotes "ardent embracing" or "wrestling." There is no doubt that he was a man who wrestled with God. Time after time throughout his prophecy we find him interceding in prayer and stretching out in faith as he seeks to bring down from the open heaven the revival that his people so desperately need. In his great prayer, Habakkuk answers the "when" of revival. He acknowledges several things that are associated with revival:

God's Sovereignty

"O Lord, . . . in the midst of the years [revive thy work]." The sovereignty of God in a spiritual awakening is always demonstrated by *the manner of His working.* God is constantly working. During His earthly ministry, Jesus could say, "My Father is working still, and I am working" (John 5:17). It is in the very nature of God's activity to continue working until the task is completed. Only the sinfulness of man hinders the progress of the divine purpose. But in spite of all that man says or does, God will finish His work. The Apostle Paul affirms this when he writes: "I am sure that he who began a good work in you will bring it to completion at the day of Jesus Christ" (Philippians 1:6).

When God works in reviving power He does so *suddenly* —"God came from Teman, and the Holy One from Mount Paran. His glory covered the heavens, and the earth was full of his praise." The Holy Spirit came suddenly at Pentecost for we read: "Suddenly there came a sound from heaven as of a rushing mighty wind. . . . And they were all filled with the Holy Spirit and began to speak with other tongues, as the Spirit gave them utterance" (Acts 2:2, 4). And following this invasion from heaven the glory of God covered the heavens and the earth was full of His praise, for with the birth of the Church, her witness passed from one city to another until the faith of the Church was "spoken of throughout the whole world" (Romans 1:8).

When God works in reviving power He also does so *searchingly*—"His brightness was like the light, rays flashed from his hand; and there he veiled his power. Before him went pestilence, and plague followed close behind." It is significant that when the Holy Spirit came at Pentecost we read that He appeared as tongues of fire upon each of the men and women gathered in the upper room (Acts 2:3). That fire symbolized God's searching ministry. It is little wonder that the preaching that followed Pentecost convicted men and women so that they had to cry out, "Brethren, what shall we do?" (Acts 2:37). Revival can never come without an exposure of and judgment on sin.

God also works *solemnly* in reviving power. Habakkuk illustrates this from the lives of David, Deborah and Joshua. He recalls how God marched through the land in indignation and trampled the heathen in anger. Already Habakkuk has pointed out in his prophecy that God is "of purer eyes than to behold evil" (Habakkuk 1:13). The prophet is only saying again that we cannot expect revival if we are not prepared to humble ourselves under the mighty hand of our God and accept His judgment on every appearance of sin.

And then God's reviving power works *savingly*—"Thou wentest forth for the salvation of thy people, for the salvation of thy anointed. Thou didst crush the head of the wicked, laying him bare from thigh to neck." In language which is both colorful and challenging, the prophet describes the mighty saving activity which follows in the wake of revival. God's purpose is always redemptive in its outworking.

In our text we also see *the manner of His timing*—"O Lord . . . in the midst of the years [revive thy work]; in the midst of the years make it known." Commentators have always found the phrase "in the midst of the years" difficult to interpret. But whatever its connotation, one thing is clear: in the sovereign workings of God we can always be sure of *the planning of God's exact moment*—"In the midst of the years make it known." When the Lord Jesus was about to leave for heaven His disciples wanted to know when and where He would restore the kingdom to His ancient people. The Master replied, "It is not for you to know the times or the seasons, which the Father hath put in his own power" (Acts 1:7). Of one thing, however, they could be certain: God works on time. At the coming of our Lord Jesus into the world God was on time: "When the fulness of the time was come, God sent forth his Son, made of a woman, made under the law" (Galatians 4:4). This was true on the occasion of the advent of the Holy Spirit, for Luke tells us:

"When the day of Pentecost was fully come. . . . suddenly there came a sound from heaven" (Acts 2:1, 2). What a relief it is to know that God has planned exactly when to send revival. Oh that we might be ready in the day of His power!

In this matter of divine timing we can be sure of *the purpose of God's express message*—"O Lord, I have heard the report of thee, and . . . I fear. . . . In the midst of the years make it known; in wrath remember mercy." God always says something definite and relevant to meet our contemporary need. We could illustrate this throughout the whole history of the Christian church, but let us start with the sixteenth century, the age of the Protestant revival known as the Reformation. The message that rang out happened to be the central word of Habakkuk—"the just shall live by his faith" (2:4). Then came the seventeenth century with the revival of Puritanism when the message was the sovereignty of God and the responsibility of man. The eighteenth century saw the first evangelical awakening, with its restatement of the simple gospel of our Lord Jesus Christ. John Wesley and George Whitefield traveled north, south, east and west in the British Isles calling on men and women to be born again and to be reconciled to God. The second evangelical awakening of the nineteenth century brought a slightly different emphasis: to evangelize the world. There was a rediscovery of the meaning of the Great Commission: to go "into all the world, and preach the gospel to every creature" (Mark 16:15). Most of the well-established evangelical societies and foreign missions were born out of that revival.

So we have seen something of the manner of God's sovereign working and timing in this unique activity of revival.

But the "when" of revival has to do also with:

Man's Extremity

"O Lord, . . . in wrath remember mercy." Here is the cry of a man in dire straits. There is a burden upon his heart; there is a sob in his voice and there are tears in his eyes. He has reached an extremity.

As I have read and reread the stories of revivals, I have found that God always visits His people when they reach *the point of desperation*. Habakkuk opens his prophecy with the words, "The oracle of God which Habakkuk the prophet saw" (1:1). Then follows a vision of the desperate condition of his people. He sees sin as high as the mountains, the law of God disregarded and the wicked surrounding the righteous. In verses 5 to 11 of that first chapter God replies to the heart-cry of the prophet and discloses what He is about to do. So backslidden and wicked were the chosen people that God had to raise up a nation worse than themselves to whip them into submission and repentance. His language is, "For lo, I am rousing the Chaldeans, that bitter and hasty nation, who march through the breadth of the earth, to seize habitations not their own" (Habakkuk 1:6).

God has had to do this again and again throughout history. And I wonder if we are not in a situation when it may well happen again. Communism, with all its strength, its sinister and subtle strategy, is infiltrating one country after another. How soon will it be before the West is overrun and the Church is driven underground and persecuted?

With such a horrifying vision before him, Habakkuk cries out with words of utter desperation:

Art thou not from everlasting, O Lord my God, my Holy One? We shall not die. O Lord, thou hast ordained them as a judgment; and thou, O Rock, hast established them for chastisement. Thou who art of purer eyes than to behold evil and canst not look on wrong, why dost thou look on faithless men, and art silent when the wicked swallows up the man more righteous than he (Habakkuk 1:12-13).

It is my conviction that we will never have revival until God has brought the Church of Jesus Christ to a point of desperation. As long as Christian people can trust religious organization, material wealth, popular preaching, shallow evangelism, and promotional drives, there will never be revival. But when confidence in the flesh is smashed, and the church comes to the realization of her desperate wretchedness, blindness and nakedness before God, then and only then will God break in.

Desperation leads us to *the point of intercession*—"I will take my stand to watch, and station myself on the tower, and look forth to see what he will say to me, and what I will answer concerning my complaint" (Habakkuk 2:1). Whether or not the "watch" was an actual watchtower with a prayer room, we do not know. What is important and plain is that Habakkuk had to shut himself up with God. There was nothing else for him to do but to watch, pray and wait until God spoke a word from heaven. Oh that God would bring us to this place of intercession! We cannot think or talk, let alone taste of revival, without intercessory prayer. Indeed, the ultimate reason for an unrevived church is the sin of prayerlessness. Certainly there are individuals who are praying for revival, and God is graciously meeting them in personal blessing in their need; but where are the prayer groups, where are the companies of intercessors, where are the churches that are united in an agonizing cry that God would open the heavens and come down and cause the mountains of hindrance and sin and unbelief to melt before His presence? There is only one thing that will save us in this hour of desperation and that is prayer.

When Habakkuk prayed with this urgency God gave him a twofold vision. First, *the vision of the sinfulness of man.* From Habakkuk 2:3 through 2:19 God describes to His servant the utter sinfulness of man by pronouncing five terrifying woes. Such is the character of this unveiling of man's desperate need that Habakkuk himself is brought to the depths of despair. But this is always God's method; until we ourselves understand heaven's pronouncement upon human sinfulness we shall never be serious enough in our praying for revival.

Second, there was *the vision of the holiness of God*—"But the Lord is in his holy temple; let all the earth keep silence before him" (Habakkuk 2:20). Because man is what he is in his native defilement, he can only understand his sinfulness in the light of God's holiness. We see this concept repeated again and again in holy Scripture. Think, for instance, of Isaiah. We find him first pronouncing woes upon all and sundry, until he catches a vision of the holiness of God in Chapter 6. Then he bursts out, "Woe is me! For I am lost; for I am a man of unclean lips, and I dwell in the midst of a people of unclean lips; for my eyes have seen the King, the Lord of hosts!" (Isaiah 6:5). Here man's extremity brings him to a point of desperation and intercession because of human sinfulness and divine holiness.

Once again, the "when" of revival has to do with:

Faith's Opportunity

"O Lord, ... in the midst of the years [revive thy work]." Until revival comes there is only one attitude for the man of God: the attitude of trust which *believes righteously*—"the just shall live by his faith" (Habakkuk 2:4). The Apostle Paul says the same thing when he writes: "For I am not ashamed of the gospel of Christ: it is the power of God for salvation to every one who has faith, to the Jew first, and also to the Greek. For in it the righteousness of God is revealed through faith for faith; as it is written, " 'He who through faith is righteous shall live' " (Romans 1:16, 17).

One of the determining factors in bringing about a churchwide revival is this determination to fulfill all of God's purposes righteously in the power of the Spirit. This, of course, is not popular in our present age. Carnal Christians do not and will not understand this attitude to life. They look askance at you and say, "Why bother to live like that? Why be a martyr? Why be considered different or odd?" God have mercy on such thinking and questioning! The Word is clear: "The just shall live by his faith." It is a faith which believes righteously and *believes rejoicingly*—for though the fig tree do not blossom, nor fruit be on the vines, the produce of the olive fail and the fields yield no food the flock be cut off from the fold and there be no herd in the stalls, *yet I will rejoice in the Lord, I will joy in the God of my salvation.* God, the Lord is my strength; he makes my feet like hinds' feet, he makes me tread upon my high places.

Dr. G. Campbell Morgan says this passage is the greatest and most priceless of all prophetic poetry.

In verse 17 Habakkuk paints a picture of a country laid waste. What a description of the present-day Church! But faith can look at a hopeless situation and laugh rejoicingly and victoriously. It does not matter how barren, how wasted, how fruitless may be the life of the church—individually or corporately—God can restore and revive. Dr. Morgan points out that to translate this passage literally would almost startle us. What Habakkuk is saying here is: "I will jump for joy in the Lord. I will spin round for joy in God." This is believing rejoicingly. This is faith looking beyond the desolation of sin to the jubilation of the Spirit.

While the man of faith believes righteously and rejoicingly, his own life is *energized*—"God, the Lord, is my strength." If we study the lives of Moses, Joshua, David, Isaiah and John, we note that, despite the human outlook, God energized them to stand the strain until it was time for Him to intervene.

The man of faith is also *stabilized*—"He makes my feet like hinds' feet." The hind, or red deer, is one of the most sure-footed of animals. However dizzy the heights or precipitous the rocks, the hind is sure of its footing. When personal revival lifts the man of faith to heights of revelation and experience, he is strengthened by God's Spirit in the inner man to stand the wonder and glory of the indwelling Son of God. How welcome it is to know that he can be "steadfast, unmovable, always abounding in the work of the Lord" (I Corinthians 15:58).

And then his life is *vitalized*—"He makes me tread upon my high places." It is one thing to stand; it is another to walk. By a glorious visitation from heaven a Christian may be placed on a pinnacle of fellowship with Christ, but it is another thing to walk in that light and to continue to breathe that rarefied atmosphere of heaven. But thank God, whether it is commencement or continuance in the Christian life, the secret is the same. It is the faith of the just. The Apostle Paul puts it this way: "As ye have therefore received Christ Jesus the Lord, so walk ye in him" (Colossians 2:6).

So we have seen that waiting for *general revival* is an opportunity for enjoying *personal revival*. While we expect the sovereignty of God, the extremity of man, and the opportunity of faith to result in a church-wide movement of the Spirit, we can *each* believe righteously and rejoicingly through a faith that is energized, stabilized and vitalized by the Word of God and the Spirit of God. Only a Christian living on these terms has a right to pray: "O Lord, . . . [revive thy work]; in the midst of the years make it known; in wrath remember mercy."

5

In the fifteenth year
of the reign of Tiberius Caesar,
Pontius Pilate being governor of Judea,
and Herod being tetrarch of Galilee,
and his brother Philip
tetrarch of the region of Ituraea and Trachonitis,
and Lysanias tetrarch of Abilene,
in the high-priesthood of Annas and Caiaphas,
the word of God came to John the son of Zechariah
in the wilderness;
and he went into all the region about the Jordan,
preaching a baptism of repentance
for the forgiveness of sins.
As it is written
in the book of the words of Isaiah the prophet,
"The voice of one crying in the wilderness:
Prepare the way of the Lord, and make his paths straight.
Every valley shall be filled,
and every mountain and hill shall be brought low,
and the crooked shall be made straight,
and the rough ways shall be made smooth;
and all flesh shall see the salvation of God."

LUKE 3:1-6

The
Way
of Revival

It was 1904. All Wales was aflame. The nation had drifted far from God. The spiritual conditions were low indeed. Church attendance was poor, and sin abounded on every side.

Suddenly, like an unexpected tornado, the Spirit of God swept over the land. The churches were crowded, so that multitudes were unable to get in. Meetings lasted from ten in the morning until twelve at night. Three definite services were held each day. Evan Roberts was the human instrument, but there was very little preaching. Singing, testimony and prayer were the chief features. There were no hymn books, they had learned the hymns in childhood; no choir, for everybody sang; no collection, and no advertising.

Nothing had ever come over Wales with such far-reaching results. Infidels were converted; drunkards, thieves and gamblers saved; and thousands reclaimed to respectability. Confessions of awful sins were heard on every side. Old debts were paid. The theater had to leave for want of patronage. Mules in coal mines refused to work, being unused to kindness! In five weeks, twenty thousand people joined the churches.

In this graphic manner, Dr. Oswald Smith tells us what happened when God swept through a country in revival blessing. Is it any wonder that we long to see another out-pouring of God's Spirit? It is just here, however, that we must remind ourselves that such a longing must be tempered with an understanding of the costly way of revival before we can see the salvation of God! That great reformer and revivalist, John the Baptist, put it this way: "Prepare the way of the Lord, make his paths straight. Every valley shall be filled, and every mountain and hill shall be brought low, and the crooked shall be made straight, and the rough ways shall be made smooth; and all flesh shall see the salvation of God." With these words he summed up the conditions that will always determine the opportunity for God to work. If revival in terms of the full salvation of God is to be seen, we must give attention to:

The Challenge

In the annals of oriental history, when an emperor or king was due to pass through the country, men were sent to prepare a highway for him. Isaiah and John borrow that metaphor to dramatize God's challenge to revival. And so the word rings out, "Prepare the way of the Lord." Now if we are to face this challenge we must first find the spiritual principles and then apply them to our individual lives.

When God tells us to "prepare the way of the Lord," He is instructing us to be a means of access through which Christ can reach others. So many of us are *obstructions* to Christ, and not *ways*. Oh that we might be like the early

Christians who were known as "the Way"! In the Acts of the Apostles, Luke employed this term six times to identify the true followers of Christ. Even a demon-possessed girl had to exclaim, concerning Paul and Silas, "These men . . . show us . . . the way of salvation" (Acts 16:17).

Can this be said of your life? Is your life a way of *prayer?* —what the writer to the Hebrews calls "the way into the sanctuary" (Hebrews 9:8)? When people encounter you, are they ushered at once into the presence of God? Do other Christians find it easy to pray with you, or is your life a distraction from prayer?

Is your life a way of *life*—"a new and living way" (Hebrews 10:20)? Jesus dedicated that way of life so that we might share it with Him. God's purpose for each believer is that he might "reign in life by one, Jesus Christ" (Romans 5:17). Paul knew something of that experience when he wrote, "For to me to live is Christ" (Philippians 1:21); and again: "Christ . . . is our life" (Colossians 3:4). May the Lord deliver us from merely existing and bring us into the real joy of living.

Is your life a way of *holiness*—"the way of righteousness" (II Peter 2:21)? Holiness is not the privilege of an "aristocracy of heaven"; rather, it is the divine expectation and standard of everyone who bears the name of Christ. The Bible reminds us that "this is the will of God, even your sanctification," and that we have not been "called . . . unto uncleanness, but unto holiness" (I Thessalonians 4:3, 7). In short, God says: "Be ye holy; for I am holy" (I Peter 1:15-16). Oh for the ambition of the saintly Robert Murray McCheyne who made it his constant prayer and ambition to be a holy man!

Is your life a way of *love*—the "more excellent way" (I Corinthians 12:31)? We have only to study a passage like I Corinthians 13 to recognize that to have everything else and to lack love is to be and to do nothing. It is said that Dr. Andrew Murray read this song of love every day on his knees before he attempted to preach or to serve his Lord. The command is clear: "Prepare the way of the Lord"; that is to say, become such a way of prayer, of life, of holiness and of love that all men may see the salvation of God worked out in you.

The Conditions

"Every valley shall be filled, and every mountain and hill shall be brought low, and the crooked shall be made straight, and the rough ways shall be made smooth." John's mission was to prepare the way of the Lord by spiritually fulfilling all the conditions for His coming—filling all the "valleys," leveling the "mountains," straightening the "ways of crookedness" and smoothing out the "rough places." And if we are to prepare the way of the Lord we too must face up to God's conditions.

First, *the valleys of defeat must be filled*—"Every valley shall be filled." Valleys are depressions and divisions in the earth's surface, and as such symbolize aspects of defeat in the believer's life. Their number is legion, but the inner defeats can be recognized by the fact that they keep the Christian in a state of depression. Some well-known ones are temper, jealousy, bitterness, resentment, moodiness, slavish fear and the inferiority complex. Then there are outward divisions. We all recognize them: exclusivism, sectarianism and obscurantism. In a word, anything that tends to break up the unity of the Spirit in the bond of peace. How tired we are of the exclusivism which never welcomes nor extends fellowship to Christians outside its own circle; the sectarianism which claims to be the whole, while it is only a small part of the Body of Christ, and the obscurantism which refuses to see the other man's point of view, and pronounces judgment without justification. Are you defeated by these valleys in your life? Remember, they must be filled up if the way is to be prepared for revival and salvation.

You may well ask, "How can the valleys in my life be filled?" The answer is, "By the Holy Spirit." The Word of

God exhorts us to "be filled with the Spirit" (Ephesians 5:18). It is only when the Holy Spirit fills the life of a believer that the depressions are mastered and the divisions are mended.

Second, *the mountains of disbelief must be leveled*—"Every mountain and hill shall be brought low." These mountains speak of disbelief. It was to illustrate the presence of such disbelief in the hearts of His disciples that Jesus used the Hebrew figure of speech, "removing mountains by faith." The mountains were not the objective, material ones, but the subjective, moral ones (Matthew 17:20)—the mountains in your life and mine that hold back the blessing. Jesus said that there was only one way to level such mountains of disbelief and that was and is to exercise "faith as a grain of mustard seed," to acknowledge, deliberately and honestly, our utter smallness, weakness and uselessness apart from God.

Unbelief springs from pride, and until we are humbled God can never exalt us in blessing. "God opposes the proud, but gives grace to the humble." So, Peter says, "Humble yourselves therefore under the mighty hand of God, that in due time he may exalt you" (I Peter 5:5-6). If we are not prepared to humble ourselves, God has to do it, and it is a fearful thing to have to fall into the hands of the living God. One of the most sobering chapters of the Bible is Daniel 4, the story of a man called Nebuchadnezzar who lifted up himself in pride before God, claiming that he had brought about his own greatness and fame. He could say, "Is not this great Babylon, which I have built by my mighty power as a royal residence ... for the glory of my majesty?" But the narrative records that

> while the words were still in the king's mouth, there fell a voice from heaven, "O King Nebuchadnezzar, to you it is spoken: The kingdom has departed from you, and you shall be driven from among men, and your dwelling shall be with the beasts of the field; and you shall be made to

eat grass like an ox; and seven times shall pass over you, until you have learned that the Most High rules the kingdom of men and gives it to whom he will." Immediately the word was fulfilled upon Nebuchadnezzar. He was driven from among men, and ate grass like an ox, and his body was wet with the dew of heaven till his hair grew as long as eagles' feathers, and his nails were like birds' claws (Daniel 4:31-33).

After seven years, having learned his lesson and being restored to sanity and dignity, Nebuchadnezzar was able to say, "Now I . . . praise and extol and honor the King of heaven; for all his works are right and his ways are just; and *those who walk in pride he is able to abase*" (v. 37).

Third, *the crooked ways of dishonesty must be straightened* —"The crooked shall be made straight." The dishonesties of life must be faced. Think, for a moment, of the dishonesty of lying; that is, any species of deliberate deception. How many times a day do you lie in thought, word or deed? Then there is the dishonesty of hypocrisy—pretending to be what you are not in your prayer, confession, testimony and life. Another serious dishonesty is that of robbing God of energy, by means of misspent money and squandered hours. These crooked ways of dishonesty must be straightened, and the time to do it is *now*. The Bible says, "If we confess our sins, he is faithful and just, and will forgive our sins and cleanse us from all unrighteousness" (I John 1:9). Will you confess and forsake lying, hypocrisy, and dishonesty in your life? This is the way of revival.

Fourth, *the rough places of dislocation must be made smooth* —"The rough ways shall be made smooth." The word "dislocation" means "to make the strata discontinuous," or "to be out of place," and this is most suggestive, for among other things it raises a number of questions: Is your personal life out of place or out of adjustment with the will of God? Nobody else can answer this but God and yourself. Think about the kind of life you live behind closed doors when you are away from the crowd. Are you out of adjustment to the will of God in relation to your family life? What about the husband/wife relationship? Husband, are you lovingly considerate of your wife? Wife, are you lovingly submissive to your husband? What about the parent/child relationship? Parents, are you bringing up your children in the nurture and admonition of the Lord, not provoking them to anger or losing their respect through lack of anointed authority, example and precept? Children, are you obeying your parents in the Lord by respecting your father and mother?

Are you out of adjustment to the will of God in relation to your church life? Do you pray for your minister? Are you in harmony with fellow elders, deacons and members within the fellowship of your local church? Are you fulfilling your obligations in terms of attendance, service, giving, witness and burden-bearing?

Then there is your social life. Are you out of adjustment to the will of God in this regard? Who are your friends—schismatic Christians who are walking in a disorderly fashion? Perhaps you have never read the Word which says, "If any one refuses to obey what we say . . . note that man, and have nothing to do with him, that he may be ashamed" (II Thessalonians 3:14).

Concerning the world, James warns us, "Whosoever therefore will be a friend of the world is the enemy of God" (James 4:4); and again:

> Do not be mismated with unbelievers. For what partnership have righteousness and iniquity? Or what fellowship has light with darkness? What accord has Christ with Belial? Or what has a believer in common with an unbeliever? Therefore come out from them, and be separate from them, says the Lord, and touch nothing unclean; then I will welcome you (II Corinthians 6:14, 15, 17).

These principles apply also to your business life. God

alone knows what might happen in the professional, commercial and industrial areas of our national life if He truly visited us with revival. What adjustments would be made!

During a time of spiritual awakening in Africa we are told that the police authorities were astounded at the genuine repentance and restitution that was made not only by converts, but by backsliders who were now restored to the Lord. The *Daily Dispatch* of East London, South Africa listed the following articles returned by repentant believers:

80 sheets, 25 blankets, 24 jackets, 34 trousers, 11 overcoats, 6 women's coats, 25 dresses, 27 skirts, 50 shirts, 22 bedspreads, 64 hats, 23 towels, 1 table, 4 chairs, 50 pillow slips, 15 scissors, 5 hairclippers, 9 wallets, 4 cameras, 4 wrist watches, 3 revolvers and ammunition, 30 tumblers and an assortment of jewelry, tools, cigarette lighters, crockery, cutlery, boots and shoes, pressure stoves, frying pans, lanterns, and safety razors.

During a similar religious awakening in the city of Belfast, under the ministry of W. P. Nicholson, there was such a spirit of repentance and restitution abroad that workers at a well-known shipyard returned sufficient material to the authorities to build and equip a sizable machine shed!

So we are bound to ask in these days of unprincipled business methods and neglected ethics, "Are you out of adjustment in relation to your business life?" Until you get right with God He will neither hear you nor bless you. Whatever the area of maladjustment, we must recall the solemn words of David, "If I had cherished iniquity in my heart, the Lord would not have listened" (Psalm 66:18).

There is only one way to be readjusted to the will of God. It is summed up for us in the words of our risen Lord in His address to the church at Ephesus: "Remember . . . from what you have fallen, repent and do the works you did at first" (Revelation 2:5).

These are certainly four heavy demands, but they constitute the essential conditions for preparing the way of the Lord. This is the way of revival. Nothing else will do.

The Consequences

"All flesh shall see the salvation of God." Look at Luke 2:30; you will notice that the salvation of God is embodied in a Person, the Lord Jesus Christ Himself. When godly Simeon lifted the infant Christ into his arms, he declared, "Lord, now lettest thou thy servant depart in peace, according to thy word: For mine eyes have seen thy salvation" (Luke 2:29-30). Revival is not just an idea; still less is it mere emotion or excitement. Revival is ultimately Christ Himself, seen, felt, heard, living, active, moving in and through His body on earth. He can only be seen by all flesh when the conditions are fulfilled. The way must be prepared and then all flesh shall see the salvation of God. Notice what this means.

First, *unlimited blessing*—"All flesh." In these two words God catches us up into His worldwide vision. He delivers us from a narrow, parochial, "four-walled" outlook. Instead of being restricted to "our little flock," our interests and blessing reach out to all flesh.

Second, *unmistakable blessing*—"All flesh *shall see*." There are always "signs following" when the risen Savior has the right of way through individuals and churches. There is no mistaking it when God starts to work, for men and women are either antagonized by, or attracted to, but never neutralized by Christ. And when this happens there is no need to hide behind the well-known cliche: "Eternity alone will reveal the results."

Third, there is *unspeakable blessing*—"All flesh shall see *the salvation of God*." This, as we have already observed, is the Lord Jesus Christ Himself, God's "unspeakable gift" —glorified and magnified among men. So the challenge rings out: "Prepare the way of the Lord.... and all flesh shall see the salvation of God." Accept the challenge, fulfill the conditions, then praise God for the consequences!

By My Spirit, by Jonathan Goforth, is the story of a great revival which swept Korea and China in 1906-1907. The blessing began when a man was ready to prepare the way of the Lord at any cost. The man's name was Goforth. The moment of truth in his life was when he came across a statement by Charles Finney to the effect that it was useless for Christians to expect revival simply by asking for it, without bothering to fulfill the laws which govern spiritual blessing. As soon as Goforth read these words, he said, "If Finney's right, then I am going to find out what these laws are and obey them, no matter what it costs." What do you think was the first law he discovered?—the very one he was not prepared to obey! It involved being reconciled to a fellow-missionary! But God bound him to that law until he put things right. When he did, the clouds burst and revival flooded his life and everyone he touched.

The vital question which arises out of this story is: What law of spiritual revival are you disobeying? Can you say, and mean it:

> *Savior I yield, long to be healed*
> *Praying Thee now to receive me:*
> *Searching my heart, bid to depart*
> *Everything there that would grieve Thee.*
> R. Hudson Pope

6

And when they had entered, they went up
to the upper room, where they were staying,
Peter and John and James and Andrew,
Philip and Thomas, Bartholomew and Matthew,
James the son of Alphaeus and Simon the Zealot
and Judas the son of James.
All these with one accord devoted themselves
to prayer, together with the women and Mary
the mother of Jesus, and with his brothers.
When the day of Pentecost had come,
they were all together in one place.
And suddenly a sound came from heaven like
the rush of a mighty wind, and it filled all
the house where they were sitting.
And there appeared to them tongues as of fire,
distributed and resting on each one of them.
And they were all filled with the Holy Spirit and began
to speak in other tongues, as the Spirit
gave them utterance.
Now when they heard this they were cut to the heart,
and said to Peter and the rest of the apostles,
"Brethren, what shall we do?"
And Peter said to them, "Repent, and be baptized
every one of you in the name of Jesus Christ
for the forgiveness of your sins; and you shall receive
the gift of the Holy Spirit."
So those who received his word were baptized,
and there were added that day
about three thousand souls.

ACTS 1:13-14; 2:1-4, 37-38, 41

The
Wind
of Revival

George Ryga, in an article excerpted from his book, *Beyond the Crimson Morning,* tells of his visit to the Ming tombs near Peking in China. Of the thirteen grave sites, only one has been excavated and opened to the public.

When an emperor was buried, living slaves sealed his remains along with his horses, pet animals, household staff and personal possessions from the inside. When the first "palace of death" was opened, so the guide who was personally involved in the excavation told Mr. Ryga, "there was a violent rush of air from behind us—a wind-howling for a long moment as the air was sucked into the tomb. I saw people and animals, the expressions on their faces still distinct, lying where they fell or had lain to die. But when the air of the outside world touched them, they broke into dust, as did the clothes they wore. The skins of the animals also collapsed. In a moment, it was all over."

What would happen if "the Breath of Heaven," the Spirit of the living God, struck some of our churches? Pentecost will always be associated with the wind of God. Luke dramatically describes the moment and movement of that wind in the familiar word: "When the day of Pentecost had come, they were all together in one place. And suddenly a sound came from heaven like the rush of a mighty wind, and it filled all the house where they were sitting."

Again and again throughout Scripture the sovereign operation of the Holy Spirit is compared to the wind. Think, for instance, of the words of God to the prophet Exekiel when He commanded him: "Prophesy unto the wind, prophesy, son of man, and say to the wind, Thus saith the Lord God; Come from the four winds, O breath, and breathe upon these slain, that they may live" (Ezekiel 37:9).

We love to recall that evening scene when Jesus talked with the puzzled theologian, Nicodemus. To make His point with regard to the work of the Holy Spirit within the **human personality, Jesus used a metaphor of the wind. As He was speaking, light evening breezes were probably** playing on their faces or sighing in the trees, and the Lord said, "The wind blows where it wills, and you hear the sound of it, but you do not know whence it comes or whither it goes; so it is with every one who is born of the Spirit" (John 3:8).

The wind of God's Spirit, the "wind of revival," blows suddenly, searchingly and sovereignly. I once heard Dr. G. Campbell Morgan say: "We cannot organize revival, but we can set our sails to catch the wind from heaven when God chooses to blow upon His people once again." What do we mean by "setting our sails"? I want to suggest, from the verses before us, that setting our sails for the wind of revival involves preparation, supplication and expectation.

Preparation

"When the day of Pentecost had come, they were all together in one place." Before He went to the cross, the Lord Jesus told His disciples to go to Jerusalem and wait there until they were endued with power from on high. His actual words were: "Behold, I send the promise of my Father upon you; but stay in the city [of Jerusalem], until you are clothed with power from on high" (Luke 24:49). And in obedience to that command they went into the city, to an upper room, to wait upon God. In every sense of the word this was a period of preparation. It involved *a oneness of mind* —"They were all with one accord in one place." Eleven times in the New Testament and on ten occasions in the book of the Acts we read that they "were of one accord." This unity of mind seems to be an essential factor in the preparation for the wind of revival.

Some time ago I read through Dr. Edwin Orr's *Second Evangelical Awakening in Britain*. In this magnificent work he tells how revival swept the British isles over one hundred years ago. Analyzing the substance of his entire treatment, I came to the conclusion that two indispensable conditions for revival are unity and prayer. In the beautiful Psalm 133 we read: "Behold, how good and how pleasant it is for brethren to dwell together in unity!" Having stated that fact, the psalmist goes on to say, "It is like the precious ointment upon the head, that ran down upon the beard, even Aaron's beard: that went down to the skirts of his garments." Then changing the analogy, the writer continues, "As the dew of Hermon, and as the dew that descended upon the mountains of Zion: for there the Lord commanded the blessing, even life for evermore."

What is the Holy Spirit saying to us in this psalm? It is that if we want the oil of fragrance, the dew of freshness, and the fullness of blessing that come with a heaven-sent revival, it will be only as we dwell together in unity! Remember that high priestly prayer of our Lord when He looked into His Father's face and said, "I . . . pray. . . . that they may all be one; even as thou, Father, art in me, and I in thee, that they also may be in us" (John 17:20, 21). It is only when Christians come together in oneness that the wind of revival begins to blow upon the church—and God's presence and power are sensed and seen among His people.

In this work of preparation there was also *an openness of heart.* A self-examination was carried out in that upper room. They rehearsed from the Scriptures and their own experience the tragic story of Judas, the traitor in the camp, the man who ministered with them, who walked with the Savior, who held the treasury, and yet whose heart was not right before God. In their attempt to find a successor to him, they prayed, "Lord, who knowest the hearts of all men, show which one of these two thou hast chosen to take the place in this ministry and apostleship from which Judas turned aside, to go to his own place" (Acts 1:24-25). It was a prayer for examination and for judgment. There was an openness of heart, and God will never send revival while there is sin unconfessed, and hearts are closed to the blaze of His glory and to the light that reveals evil.

So we see that preparation involves a oneness of mind and an openness of heart, but it also calls for *an obedience of will.* Those 120 disciples gathered in the upper room were fulfilling the command of the Master who said, "Stay in the city [of Jerusalem], until you are clothed with power from on high" (Luke 24:49). Obedience is always a prerequisite to the filling and flooding of the Holy Spirit. The Word tells us that the Spirit is given to those who obey Him (Acts 5:32).

Are you longing for revival? Are you praying for the wind of God to blow upon the Church of Jesus Christ? Then set your sails by way of preparation to catch that heavenly breeze! Remember that it will involve a oneness of mind, an openness of heart and an obedience of will.

Supplication

"These all continued with one accord in prayer and supplication" (Acts 1:14). There was nothing spasmodic or intermittent about their praying. On the contrary, there was *a constancy in prayer.* Prayer is rarely mentioned in the Word of God without an emphasis on continuance. Jesus said, "Men ought always to pray, and not to faint" (Luke 18:1). The Apostle Paul exhorts us to "pray without ceasing" (I Thessalonians 5:17).

Prayer is not only an activity, but an attitude of life. If we would pray always and without ceasing, then our whole life should be one of continuous prayer for whatever God would say or send. Many people imagine that prayer is the overcoming of the reluctance of God to give; whereas, in point of fact, prayer is the adjustment of our lives to God's will in order that He might be able to send the blessing He is waiting and longing to grant to His people. Bishop Lightfoot says, "It is not in the moving of the lips, but in the elevation of the heart to God that the essence of prayer consists" —and it is surely in this sense that we should put into practice the injunction to "pray without ceasing."

It is not possible for us to spend all our time with the words of prayer on our lips, but it is possible for us to be all our days in the spirit of prayer, realizing our dependence upon God for all that we have and are, realizing something of His presence with us wherever we may be, and yielding ourselves continually to Him for the doing of His will. Where there is such an inward state, it will find outward expression in verbal prayer, and in this connection we should notice the frequent ejaculatory prayers throughout Paul's letters. Prayer was so natural and so continual with the great Apostle that it found its way inevitably into his correspondence (Dr. Leon Morris).

A unity in prayer—"These all continued with one accord in prayer" (Acts 1:14). We have already spoken of the importance of unity in mind and in heart, but this must be carried into our prayer life as well. Jesus said, "If two of you shall agree on earth as touching any thing that they shall ask, it shall be done for them of my Father which is in heaven" (Matthew 18:19). Have you ever put that promise to the test?

Dr. James Little tells the story of the 1857 revival in New York City and area. There was a man whose soul was moved with a deep longing for an outpouring of the Spirit in that great city. The spiritual land around him was arid and parched, and his cry was, "Turn again our captivity, O Lord, as the streams in the south" (Psalm 126:4). Desiring that others should join him in concerted prayer, he displayed a little card in the window of a room on Fulton Street which read: "If anyone is interested to pray for revival, come in and join me." The first day he prayed alone. Then others began to join him, until the room became too small. The burden for revival had begun to spread—until hundreds had caught the spirit of intercession and supplication.

Four young men in County Antrim, Northern Ireland, knelt in united prayer in a schoolroom. They longed and prayed for revival, and God met them in such a way that the whole of Ireland was affected. Indeed, that was the beginning of the 1859 revival that has influenced the country ever since.

Other instances could be cited to further prove that God honors unity in prayer. But in addition to this, there must be *a fervency in prayer*—"These all continued with one accord in prayer and supplication" (Acts 1:14). Prayer has a general connotation of waiting on God, whereas the word "supplication" suggests the beseeching and petitioning aspect of intercession. It is the laying hold of the Lord which will not let go or let up until something happens. This is how Elijah prayed, and James, in citing this man of prayer, writes: "The prayer of a righteous man has great power in its effects." (James 5:16).

This kind of praying costs, for it involves fasting, discipline and persistence. Luke recorded a prayer meeting of this kind in the twelfth chapter of Acts. We read that "prayer was made without ceasing of the church unto God" for the imprisoned Peter. Such was the fervency and faithfulness of the praying that before the night was over Peter was delivered from his prison cell and released to preach again the gospel of Christ. Are we prepared to set our sails by this ministry of supplication with constancy, unity and fervency? Only then can we expect to hear the mighty rushing wind from heaven.

Expectation

When the day of Pentecost had come, they were all together in one place. And suddenly a sound came from heaven like the rush of a mighty wind, and it filled all the house where they were sitting. And there appeared to them tongues as of fire, distributed and resting on each one of them. And they were all filled with the Holy Spirit and began to speak in other tongues, as the Spirit gave them utterance (Acts 2:1-4).

We can pray all night and all day throughout the coming weeks, and appear outwardly enthusiastic, but if there is no expectancy in our hearts there will be no blessing. A man said to me some time ago that he believed that God could stem the tide of evil, but he didn't have the faith to expect it. It never occurred to him that this was a contradiction of terms.

True expectation calls for *a faith that believes.* Jesus had said to His disciples, "I send the promise of my Father upon you" (Luke 24:49). They believed the promise. Indeed, one can sense the spirit of expectancy which characterized them as they knelt in prayer in that upper room. We also must exercise the faith which believes. Jesus said, "All things, whatsoever ye shall ask in prayer, believing, ye shall receive" (Matthew 21:22). James reminds us that we are to "ask in faith, nothing wavering: for he that wavereth is like a wave of the sea driven with the wind and tossed. For let not that man think that he shall receive any thing of the Lord" (James 1:6-7). "Faith cometh by hearing, and hearing by the word of God," declares the Apostle Paul (Romans 10:17).

There are a multitude of promises in the Old and New Testaments that give us the confidence to believe that God is waiting to send revival. One example is: "Be patient," says the Apostle James, "unto the coming of the Lord. Behold, the husbandman waiteth for the precious fruit of the earth, and hath long patience for it, until he receive the early and latter rain" (James 5:7). Do we believe that the latter rain of revival is to fall before Jesus comes back again? The promise is clear enough, but is our faith strong enough? Is it a faith which *believes?*

Expectancy also calls for *a faith that receives*—"They were all filled with the Holy Spirit." God fills only the hearts and lives of those who have a receiving faith. Have you received this fullness? God's purpose for our lives is continuous revival, and continuous revival is equated with the continuous fullness of the Holy Spirit. When we are first converted the word to us is: "Repent, and be baptized every one of you in the name of Jesus Christ for the remission of sins, and ye shall *receive the gift of the Holy Spirit*." From that point on the relevant exhortation is Ephesians 5:18, "Be filled with the Spirit." Have we the faith to receive the fullness which God is waiting to pour out?

Expectation further calls for *a faith that achieves*. We read: "They were all filled with the Holy Spirit, and began to speak . . . as the Spirit gave them utterance. . . . there were added that day about three thousand souls." Filled with the Holy Spirit, speaking with fearlessness, they stepped out to achieve results for God. And their expectation was not unrewarded. A large city was shaken, a great crowd was challenged and three thousand souls were converted in one day. Their whole ministry carried a relevance, an authority and a conviction such as men and women had never before witnessed. What happened on the day of Pentecost continued to happen through succeeding days and weeks, for we read that "the Lord added to the church daily those who were being saved" (Acts 2:47); that is to say, men and women got right with God; not only on Sundays or on special preaching occasions, but every day, in homes, in the synagogue, in the market place and wherever unconverted men and women came into contact with those Spirit-filled, revived men and women.

So we have seen that our part in revival is to adjust the sails of our spiritual life to catch the first breeze that comes from heaven. Such adjustment involves preparation, supplication and expectation; or to put it in the words of Bessie P. Head:

> *O Breath of Life, come sweeping through us,*
> *Revive Thy Church with life and pow'r;*
> *O Breath of Life, come, cleanse, renew us,*
> *And fit Thy Church to meet this hour.*
>
> *O Wind of God, come bend us, break us,*
> *Till humbly we confess our need;*
> *Then in Thy tenderness remake us,*
> *Revive, restore, for this we plead.*
>
> *O Breath of Love, come breathe within us,*
> *Renewing thought and will and heart;*
> *Come, Love of Christ, afresh to win us,*
> *Revive Thy Church in every part.*
>
> *O Heart of Christ, once broken for us,*
> *'Tis there we find our strength and rest;*
> *Our broken contrite hearts now solace,*
> *And let Thy waiting Church be blest.*
>
> *Revive us, Lord! Is zeal abating*
> *While harvest fields are vast and white?*
> *Revive us, Lord, the world is waiting,*
> *Equip Thy Church to spread the light.*

7

And as they were speaking to the people,
the priests and the captains of the temple
and the Sadducees came upon them. . . .
Now when they saw the boldness of Peter
and John, and perceived that they were uneducated,
common men, they wondered;
and they recognized that they had been with Jesus. . . .
They conferred with one another,
saying, "What shall we do with these men?
For that a notable sign
has been performed through them
is manifest to all the inhabitants of Jerusalem,
and we cannot deny it.
But in order that it may spread no further
among the people, let us warn them to speak no more
to any one in this name."
So they called them and charged them not to speak
or teach at all in the name of Jesus.
But Peter and John answered them,
"Whether it is right in the sight of God
to listen to you rather than to God, you must judge;
for we cannot but speak of what we have seen and heard.
And when they had further threatened them,
they let them go, finding no way to punish them,
because of the people;
for all men praised God for what had happened.

ACTS 4:1, 13, 15-21

The *Wake* of Revival

Something of such far-reaching consequence had taken place in Jerusalem that everyone in the city was aware of it. The Spirit of God had been poured out upon a handful of men and women, and, as a result, the very foundations of hell had been shaken. Never had such miraculous happenings been witnessed. On the day of Pentecost three thousand souls had been added to the infant church. A few days later five thousand more were converted, and then still another five thousand until Luke, in his record, had to give up counting and by way of reporting used the adjective "myriad" to represent the multitudes who were turning to the Lord. Nothing quite like it has ever happened since. The enemies of the cross had to stand back and say,

"What shall we do with these men? . . . that it may spread

no further among the people, let us warn them to speak no more to any one in this name." So they called them and charged them not to speak or teach at all in the name of Jesus. But Peter and John answered them, "Whether it is right in the sight of God to listen to you rather than to God, you must judge; for we cannot but speak of what we have seen and heard."

The antagonists of the gospel had to acknowledge that "something was spreading—and spreading fast." Little did they know that it was the "wake" of revival.

This is our urgent need today, and we must not be satisfied with anything less. Our study of God's Word, our ministry in prayer, our holiness of living and our devotion in service must all be directed to this end.

The Secret of Spreading Revival

I believe the secret is summed up in that most significant little statement—"they had been with Jesus." Revival in the last analysis—whether praying, praising or preaching—is Jesus. It is the manifestation of the glory, power and blessing of the Son of God among His people. It must always be characterized by the place and prominence it gives to the person, office and work of our matchless Savior.

The early disciples had been with Jesus and the outside world could not fail to recognize it. Their lives were Christ-captured, Christ-centered and Christ-controlled. In his writings Luke tells us, "When they saw the boldness of Peter and John, and perceived that they were uneducated, common men, they wondered; and they recognized that they had been with Jesus." The Apostle Paul testifies of the same experience when he writes, "For to me to live [or, life itself] is Christ" (Philippians 1:21). Thus, wherever the apostles went, and whatever they said or did, Christ was seen and heard and felt.

The Lord Jesus Christ always creates an issue. That was true of His human life on earth. Study His contact with individuals, groups or even large crowds, and you will notice that He never neutralized. He always antagonized or attracted them. When He spoke, people either believed on Him or they picked up stones to stone Him. In the Gospel of John particularly, we come across words like this: "There was a division therefore again among the Jews for these sayings. And many of them said, He hath a devil, and is mad; why hear ye him? Others said, These are not the words of him that hath a devil. Can a devil open the eyes of the blind?" (John 10:19-21). We must never forget that He is the same Lord who indwells us by the power of the Holy Spirit and the same power should characterize our lives.

The disciples had been with Jesus. He was *the subject of their confession*—"They [spoke of him with] boldness." The word "boldness" suggests the idea of fluency and freedom of speech. Their confession was fearless. "When we read the speech of Peter, we must remember to whom it was spoken, and when we do remember that, it becomes one of the world's great demonstrations of courage. It was spoken to an audience of the wealthiest, the most intellectual and the most powerful in the land, and yet Peter, the Galilean fisherman, stands before them rather as their judge than as their victim. But further, this was the very crowd which had condemned Jesus to death. Peter knew it, and he knew that at this moment he was taking his life in his hands. There are two kinds of courage. There is the reckless courage which goes on scarcely aware of the dangers it is facing. There is the far higher, cool, calculated courage which knows the peril in which it stands and which will not be daunted. It was that second courage that Peter demonstrated to men. When Achilles, the great warrior of the Greeks, was told that if he went out to battle he would surely die, he answered in the immortal sentence, 'Nevertheless, I am for going on.' Peter, in that moment, knew the peril in which he stood; nevertheless, he, too, was for going on." (Dr. William Barclay). We read that

Peter, filled with the Holy Spirit, said to them, "Rulers of the people and elders, if we are being examined today concerning a good deed done to a cripple, by what means this man has been healed, be it known to you all, and to all the people of Israel, that by the name of Jesus Christ of Nazareth, *whom you crucified,* whom God raised from the dead, by him this man is standing before you well" (Acts 4:8-10).

Did you ever read of such fearlessness? And remember, this is the man who crouched and cringed at the laugh of a servant girl who accused him of being associated with Jesus on that fateful night before the crucifixion.

Something had happened to this man. He was full of the Holy Spirit and with the fullness came a truly remarkable freedom and fearlessness of confession. That is why revival spread; that is why those men left a spiritual wake behind them wherever they went or preached. It was a fearless confession, but it was also a faithful confession. It summed up everything. Peter could say, "This is the stone which was rejected by you builders, but which has become the head of the corner. And there is salvation in no one else, for there is no other name under heaven given among men by which we must be saved" (Acts 4:11-12).

You cannot imagine anything more faithful to the truth. Peter was narrowing the salvation of God right down to one gospel, one name, one person—the Lord Jesus. In his words there is no sense of embarrassment; no apology for dragging religion into his sermon; no attempt at rationalizing the plain and simple fact that Jesus is the only Savior of men. And do not forget, all this was spoken to the very same members of the Sanhedrin who had condemned Jesus to death fifty days earlier!

With the subject of their confession there was *the strength of their conviction*—"Now when they saw the boldness of Peter and John, and perceived that they were uneducated, common men, they wondered." Bishop Charles John Ellicott points out that "the first of the two words means, literally, unlettered. Looking to the special meaning of the 'letters' of 'Scriptures' of the Jews, from which the scribes took their name (*grammateis,* from *grammata*), it would convey, as used here the sense of 'not having been educated as a scribe, not having studied the Law and other sacred writings.' This word does not occur elsewhere in the New Testament. The second word means, literally, a private person, one without special office or calling or the culture which they imply: what in English might be called a 'common man.' " The Bishop goes on to state that later this word acquired the sense of "an idiot."

Christians have always been attacked by intellectuals and professionals, but God has always had His answer through His chosen instruments. Even Paul recognized this when he said,

> Ye see your calling, brethren, how that not many wise men after the flesh, not many mighty, not many noble, are called: But God hath chosen the foolish things of the world to confound the wise; and God hath chosen the weak things of the world . . . and things which are despised, hath God chosen, yea, and things which are not despised, hath God chosen, yea, and things which are not, to bring to nought things which are: That no flesh should glory (I Corinthians 1:26-29).

So God used Peter and John to confound the intellectuals and professionals of his day. It is true, of course, that though ordinary fishermen, they had been under the discipline, example and instruction of the greatest Teacher the world has ever known. Notwithstanding this, however, carnal intellectualism and professionalism still found fault. Think of what the religious leaders said of Jesus Himself when they asked, "How is it that this man has learning, when he has never studied?" (John 7:15). And remember what the carnal Corinthians had to say about the Apostle

Paul: "For his letters...are weighty and powerful: but his bodily presence is weak, and his speech contemptible" (II Corinthians 10:10).

In a word, the criticism of Peter and John was that they were neither intellectual nor professional. "But hasn't that always been the story?" says Master Trappe, quoting Tertullian. In the days of the early church the world caricatured the God of the Christian with an ass's head and a book in His hand because they maintained it was a religion without learning. But in spite of this hostile reaction Jesus was the subject of their confession, the strength of their conviction, and *the substance of their communion*—"They recognized that they had been *with* Jesus." Jesus was the center and secret of an indivisible fellowship. He was the point of integration for their common life, love and loyalty.

This then was the secret of the spreading revival, and in the wake of this spiritual movement thousands were turning to Christ and Christianity.

The Signs of Spreading Revival

The chapter before us and indeed the whole of the Acts of the Apostles are full of such signs. The early apostles knew such an anointing upon their lives that it is recorded that "many signs and wonders were done...by [them]" (Acts 5:12).

"Signs and wonders" are an evidence of the supernatural. The problem in our day is that almost all activity can be explained in human terms. We are organized and computerized to accomplish most of what goes on in our churches. In fact, it has been said that in some places of worship the Holy Spirit could withdraw altogether and a lot of people would not know the difference. This is not only ludicrous, it is serious, and it is the essential problem of our religious life today. We have evacuated both our words and deeds of the miraculous. As a consequence, men and women around us today question the inerrancy of the Word of God, the divinity of the Son of God and the authority of the church of God.

But to return to the early church, the days were filled with signs and wonders—*miraculous events*. The astounded enemies of Christ had to ask, "What shall we do with these men? For that a notable sign has been performed through them is manifest to all the inhabitants of Jerusalem, and we cannot deny it." Revival has always been accompanied by miraculous events, because it is the function of the Holy Spirit to effect miracles. And we are still living in the age of the Spirit. Pentecost was not just a day; it was the beginning of a dispensation or age of the Church. God forgive us for trying to narrow down the operation of the Holy Spirit to our theological systems, our traditional forms, our denominational organizations and, worst of all, our deplorable unbelief. It has yet to be seen in our day what God can accomplish when men and women truly say and mean, "I believe in the Holy Spirit." Then, and only then, shall we see miraculous events taking place through the ministry of praying, preaching and healing.

Another sign was *conspicuous effects*—"And when they had further threatened them, they let them go, finding no way to punish them, because of the people; for all men praised God for what had happened." As we have already observed, thousands had been converted already and God was continuing to save. Furthermore, healings were taking place, and the whole city was being impacted by the power of the gospel so that all men glorified God for that which was done. Nothing was happening in a corner. Everybody was aware of the fact that Jesus was alive, that His name symbolized a life-transforming gospel, and that His followers were fearless witnesses to a new spiritual movement. True, there was opposition, as we have seen only too clearly, but that also is a conspicuous effect of revival.

I thrill again and again as I read the language of Peter and John as they stand arraigned before the Sanhedrin: "Whether it is right in the sight of God to listen to you rather than to God, you must judge; for we cannot but speak of what we have seen and heard." Here were men who knew that they were on the victory side. Nothing was going to hold them back. I can almost hear them saying one to another, "By the power of the Holy Spirit we have taken the metropolis of Jerusalem; now let us go on to the next city."

It was a question of moving forward to greater and greater exploits for God, and in the wake of the mighty revival, they left behind them innumerable men and women and boys and girls who had entered into life.

How that contrasts with the pessimism and defeatism of today. We hear it all around us from those who say that this could never happen again. And because of our unbelief even the Son of God Himself can do no mighty miracles. We have so relegated God to second place and grieved the Holy Spirit by organizational, promotional and drumbeating independence that we have lost the victorious outlook that follows in the train of the Savior's triumph. Oh, that God would turn again our captivity until we see the signs of spreading revival once again!

The Scope of Spreading Revival

In the light of the teaching of the Book of the Acts, we can sum up the scope of spreading revival in the one phrase, "the life of the Spirit." Wherever we look we find expressions which will convince even the casual reader that these early Christians were living in the Spirit. They knew *the fullness of the Spirit*—"And when they had prayed, the place in which they were gathered together was shaken; and they were all filled with the Holy Spirit" (Acts 4:31). It is important to state again that there can be no revival outside of the fullness of the Holy Spirit. Only within the scope of this spiritual fullness can there be "times of refreshing . . . from the presence of the Lord" (Acts 3:19). The question we must ask ourselves continually is, "Am I consciously, believingly, victoriously, full of the Holy Spirit?" It was because Peter was full of the Holy Spirit that he could preach for God (Acts 4:8); it was because Stephen was full of the Holy Spirit that he could suffer for God (Acts 7:55); it was because Barnabas was full of the Holy Spirit that he could exhort for God (Acts 11:24); it was because Saul, who became Paul, was full of the Holy Spirit that he could rebuke for God (Acts 13:9); and so it goes right through the Acts of the Apostles.

These disciples also knew *the freedom of the Spirit*—"They were all filled with the Holy Spirit and spoke the word of God with boldness" (Acts 4:31). Earlier we noticed that this word "boldness" suggests freedom, fluency and fearlessness. But let us remember that liberty does not suggest the desire to do what you *want*. Liberty is rather the power to do what you *ought*. Liberty is not license. Therefore, the freedom of the Holy Spirit will never lead to unhealthy extremism or anything else that would dishonor the person of our Lord Jesus Christ. The freedom of the Holy Spirit is a spiritual control which contrains and restrains the individual believer or a group of believers to walk within the will of God.

Once more, these disciples knew *the fellowship of the Spirit* —"Now the company of those who believed were of one heart and soul, and no one said that any of the things which he possessed was his own, but they had everything in common" (Acts 4:32). Here was a movement of the Spirit within the whole true church of Christ. This was no splinter group activity. On the contrary, all who believed were of one heart and of one soul. If you like, it was a kind of Christian communionism in which everything was shared—"no one said that any of the things which he possessed was his own." The life and gifts and service of Christ were shared together. This was genuine participation or communion.

Here we have the scope of true revival—the fullness, freedom and fellowship of the Spirit. No wonder things were happening in the wake of this mighty spiritual movement. "Can it happen again?" you ask. The answer is, "Positively, yes," for the Holy Spirit is as powerful today as He was on the day of Pentecost. All He waits for is the Church, made up of men and women who are prepared to quit grieving Him and quenching Him in order that He might fill and overflow in revival blessing to all areas of life.

The serious problem of our age is that Christian men and women are sinning against the Holy Spirit. The Puritan, John Calvin, was right when he pointed out that the sin of Old Testament times was the rejection of Jehovah God, the sin of New Testament times was the rejection of the Son of God, and the sin of the Church age is the rejection of the Holy Spirit. There are so-called believers all over Christendom today who refuse to acknowledge the sovereignty of the Holy Spirit in individual and congregational life. These people are not living in the fullness and freedom and fellowship of the Spirit. This is why we do not know a contagious revival. But let us not be pessimistic; revival *can* come and *will* come, carrying in its wake all the blessings which are promised to us in Christ, if we are prepared to discover the secret, discern the signs and determine the scope of a heaven-sent revival.

Let us then start to pray for this in the language of Charles H. Gabriel:

> *Lord, as of old at Pentecost*
> *Thou didst Thy power display,*
> *With cleansing, purifying flame*
> *Descend on us today.*
>
> *For mighty works for Thee, prepare*
> *And strengthen every heart;*
> *Come, take possession of Thine own,*
> *And nevermore depart.*
>
> *All self consume, all sin destroy!*
> *With earnest zeal endue*
> *Each waiting heart to work for Thee;*
> *O Lord, our faith renew!*

Speak, Lord! before Thy throne we wait,
  Thy promise we believe,
And will not let Thee go until
  The blessing we receive.

8

Be patient, therefore, brethren,
until the coming of the Lord.
Behold, the farmer waits
for the precious fruit of the earth,
being patient over it until it receives
the early and the late rain.
You also be patient. Establish your hearts,
for the coming of the Lord is at hand.
Do not grumble, brethren, against one another,
that you may not be judged;
behold, the Judge is standing at the doors.
As an example of suffering and patience, brethren,
take the prophets who spoke in the name of the Lord.
Behold, we call those happy who were steadfast.
You have heard of the steadfastness of Job,
and you have seen the purpose of the Lord,
how the Lord is compassionate and merciful.

JAMES 5:7-11

The
Wait
of Revival

A Greek church father known as Clement, born about A.D. 150, informs us that James and his brother Jude were farmers. This explains why James so often uses illustrations from a farmer's life. He speaks, for instance, of the rain of seedtime, and the rain of ripening harvest. The first fell in Judea about the middle of October, after the seed was sown, and the second toward the end of April, when the ears were filling and ripening for harvest. Without those two rains the earth would have been unfruitful.

The fact that "the latter rain" is yet to fall gives me great confidence in believing that the Church is yet to witness revival, before the husbandman returns for the precious fruit of the earth, even though the world will concurrently grow more wicked, defiant and deserving of judgment.

The Promise of God Concerning Revival

"The farmer . . . being patient . . . until [the earth] receives the early and the late rain." It is both interesting and instructive to observe that God has promised the "early and latter rain" in terms of *physical fulfillment*. When the children of Israel were about to enter the land of Canaan, God said through Moses: "I will give you the rain of your land in his due season, the first rain and the latter rain, that thou mayest gather in thy corn, and thy wine, and thine oil" (Deuteronomy 11:11-14). It is clear from this passage, and a number of others, that the harvest was dependent upon the rain, and that the rain was promised by God, contingent upon obedience. When the nation followed God, there was rain, harvest and plenty. When there was a departure from the way of righteousness, then there was drought, famine and distress. We are all familiar with the story of Elijah who was commanded to pray that it might not rain, and we read in the chapter before us: "For three years and six months it did not rain on the earth. Then he prayed again and the heaven gave rain, and the earth brought forth its fruit" (vv. 17-18). Thus God taught His people that His purpose for them was "the early and latter rain"—if only they would be obedient to His Word.

But what had been true in the physical life of God's ancient people had been equally true in the spiritual life of all His people, Jew and Gentile. The promise of "early and latter rain" has a *spiritual fulfillment*—"The farmer waits . . . until [the earth] receives the early and the late rain." During Old Testament times the rain of revival fell again and again during periods of spiritual awakening and renewal throughout the history of the Jews. But when we come to the New Testament, it can be shown that Pentecost was the historical and spiritual commencement of the fall of the "early rain." Indeed, such was the outpouring of the Holy Spirit in those days that in little more than thirty years the whole of the civilized world was evangelized for Christ and the ground prepared for the final harvest.

Since then the rain of blessing has not entirely ceased. Like the occasional showers that continue to fall from October through to the latter rain of April, in Palestine, there have been downpours of revival throughout the history of the Church. Particularly has it been so since the Reformation. But now we await the final outpouring, "the latter rain." It is evident from our text that this is going to precede the coming of the Lord and, therefore, coincide with the final harvest. The Lord Jesus explained in the parable of the tares that "the harvest is the end of the world" (Matthew 13:39-41). And then He will come with His sickle to reap the precious fruit of the earth (see Revelation 14:14-16).

If this is so, then before our Savior returns we must expect the promised rain of harvest. Oh that it might begin to fall soon! If we believe that God's promise concerning the second advent of His Son must and will be fulfilled, we must also believe that He will honor His promise concerning "the latter rain" of revival.

The Purpose of God Concerning Revival

"The farmer waits for the precious fruit of the earth, being patient over it." The purpose of God in revival is *to hasten the day of the crowning harvest*—"The farmer waits for the precious fruit of the earth." The Holy Scriptures and the story of revivals show that the greatest harvesting periods in history have always coincided with the outpouring of the Holy Spirit. That there is a great harvest to reap is beyond dispute. The Master in His day said, "The harvest is plentiful, but the laborers are few; pray therefore the Lord of the harvest to send out laborers into his harvest" (Matthew 9:37-38); and again: "Do . . . not say, 'There are yet four months, then comes the harvest.' I tell you, lift up your eyes, and see how the fields are already white for harvest" (John 4:35).

If these words carried a sense of urgency about them two thousand years ago, what about today—with the shrinkage of the globe, the population explosion, and advanced methods of communicating the gospel? The only lack, the vital lack, is the pouring out of the Spirit in revival. Without it, our efforts, however modern, scientific and advanced, are of little worth.

God's purpose in revival is to hasten the crowning harvest and also *to hasten the day of the coming husbandman*—"for the coming of the Lord is at hand." The Apostle Peter expresses the same thought when he exhorts believers to "look for and hasten the coming of the day of God" (II Peter 3:12, marginal rendering).

It is one of the functions of the Holy Spirit in the believer to make him homesick for heaven. Paul puts it this way: "But we all, with open face beholding as in a glass the glory of the Lord, are changed into the same image from glory to glory, even as by the Spirit of the Lord" (II Corinthians 3:18). The more the Holy Spirit fills and transforms us, the more we become like Jesus and long for heaven.

If the early rain is necessary for the germination of the seed, the latter rain is needful for fruitbearing. If the Church would only experience a season of revival, we would see transforming changes taking place with amazing rapidity.

The Patience of God Concerning Revival

"Be patient, therefore, brethren, until the coming of the Lord. Behold, the farmer waits for the precious fruit of the earth, being patient over it. . . . You also be patient. Establish your hearts, for the coming of the Lord is at hand." The quality of patience is a divine virtue. The word signifies long-suffering and suggests brave endurance during affliction and the refusal to give way under it, even under pressure.

Patience is that holy self-restraint which enables the sufferer to refrain from hasty retaliation. Patience has nothing whatsoever to do with indifference, apathy or stoicism. Since God has promised and purposed revival, He patiently waits for it, regardless of circumstances in the world and conditions in the Church. The believer is to exercise similar patience. In fact, where there is no patience for revival there is no prayer for revival, and therefore no faith in God's promise and purpose in revival. So James draws attention to the patience of God in order that the believer might *emulate extended patience*—"You also be patient. Establish your hearts, for the coming of the Lord is at hand." God is patient; the Lord Jesus is patient; the Holy Spirit is patient; the prophets of old were patient. Concerning the latter, James says, "As an example of suffering and patience, brethren, take the prophets who spoke in the name of the Lord. Behold, we call those happy who were steadfast. You have heard of the steadfastness of Job, and you have seen the purpose of the Lord, how the Lord is compassionate and merciful."

There is hardly a prophet in the Old Testament who was not in some way an "example of suffering affliction and of patience." Stephen, in his defense before the religious leaders of his day, asked his accusers this question: "Which of the prophets have not your fathers persecuted?" (Acts 7:52).

Jesus said: "Blessed are ye, when men shall revile you, and persecute you, and shall say all manner of evil against you falsely, for my sake. Rejoice, and be exceeding glad: for great is your reward in heaven: for so persecuted they the prophets which were before you" (Matthew 5:11-12).

Perhaps the prophet that James had in mind, above all others, was Jeremiah—who later became known as *the* Prophet. Professor R. V. G. Tasker says of him:

This hypersensitive, warmhearted patriot, compelled to proclaim a succession of divine messages to his countrymen that were unpopular because they were of necessity pessimistic, who was so sympathetic towards the sufferings of others, was himself beaten, put in the stocks, imprisoned in a dungeon, and thrown into a cistern by the very men whom he would gladly have saved if such salvation had been possible, from the doom that awaited them. His life was one of almost perpetual physical and spiritual suffering, yet his demeanor throughout was such that, of all the historical characters of the Old Testament, he was the one who most foreshadowed Him Who, when He was reviled, reviled not again, and Who suffered for man's salvation the physical and spiritual agony of the cross.

Then, of course, James mentions Job. The word "patience" used of him is not the same as the word employed in the previous verses. It is a term which implies "constancy and endurance." "No English word," writes F. J. A. Hort, "is quite strong enough to express the active courage and resolution here implied."

What a familiar story is Job's record of constancy, endurance and steadfastness! To quote Professor Tasker once again:

> It is not so much the self-restraint of Job under affliction, leading him to be patient with others, that is here emphasized, for Job was very far from showing patience in this sense with his so-called comforters. What Job did, however, display in a marked degree was the determination to endure whatever might fall to his lot without losing faith in God. He believed even when he could not understand.
>
> When blow after blow had fallen upon him in rapid succession Job cried, "Naked came I out of my mother's womb, and naked shall I return thither: the Lord gave, and the Lord hath taken away; blessed be the name of the Lord" (Job 1:21). His reply to his wife when she invited him to curse God and die was, "Thou speakest as one of the foolish women speaketh. What? shall we receive good at the hand of God, and shall we not receive evil?" (Job 2:10). To "the physicians of no value" who posed as his friends, his answer was, "Though he slay me, yet will I trust in him" (Job 13:15). He was convinced that his witness was in heaven and his record with the Most High

(Job 16:19); and he knew that his Redeemer was alive (Job 19:25).

The end of the Lord was the complete vindication of Job by his Maker. Not only were his material possessions and his worldly prosperity restored to him, but he was granted a fuller understanding of the mystery of the divine purpose, and a more direct experience of the majesty and sovereignty of Almighty God, and he became capable of a greater and deeper penitence. "I have heard of thee by the hearing of the ear," he was able to cry, "but now mine eye seeth thee: Wherefore I abhor myself, and repent in dust and ashes" (Job 42:5-6). So it was that "the Lord blessed the latter end of Job more than his beginning" (Job 42:12). The God whose severity Job had for so long experienced, as his character was tested in the furnace of affliction, in the end showed Himself to be, in the words of the Psalmist quoted by James, very pitiful, and of tender mercy (Psalm 103:8).

What a call to patience this is! But before we move from this point it is important that we should note the manner in which we are to emulate extended patience. James exhorts, "You also be patient. Establish your hearts, for the coming of the Lord is at hand."

The twofold secret of maintained patience is intercession and expectation. The word for "establish" in the Septuagint is the same as that which is used for bolstering or holding up of Moses' hands (Exodus 17:12). Patience for revival can only be bolstered up by prayer. Then there is the spirit of expectation which should characterize every truly born-again soul, for the Apostle Peter reminds us that we are "begotten . . . unto a [living] hope" (I Peter 1:3). If we have that hope and believe God's promise, we can patiently wait for the glorious fulfillments of revival and the coming again of the Lord Jesus Christ.

So we are to emulate extended patience—as seen in God Himself and as reproduced in the saints who have left us "an example of suffering and patience."

But the patience of God is also designed to *deprecate exhausted patience*—"Grudge not one against another, brethren, lest ye be condemned: behold, the judge standeth before the door." The word "grudge" means "to grumble, murmur, or complain." Under the pressure of opposition, persecution and tribulation we can soon exhaust our patience—unless we are drawing freely on the resources of God. At such times as these we fall victim to the sin and spirit of grumbling, murmuring and complaining. We blame God for not answering our prayers for revival, and then we criticize one another for being hindrances to blessing, without recognizing that we are under condemnation ourselves. The Word says that to grumble is to be condemned. Let us never forget that "the Judge is standing at the doors." He hears and knows everything; and when He comes He will judge everything. "For we must all appear before the judgment seat of Christ, so that each one may receive good or evil, according to what he has done in the body" (II Corinthians 5:10).

Let us see to it then that we never exhaust our patience and become a grumbling people. For unbelief and grumbling the children of Israel were all barred (save two men) from the promised land of blessing. It is possible to be bypassed by revival even when it comes. God save us from such a tragedy!

So we have observed that "the latter rain" of revival suggests to us the promise, purpose and patience of God concerning revival. O that we might be given the patience for the latter rain of revival which made John Newton write:

> *Saviour, visit Thy plantation,*
> *Grant us, Lord, a gracious rain!*
> *All will come to desolation,*
> *Unless Thou return again.*
> *Keep no longer at a distance,*
> *Shine upon us from on high,*

Lest, for want of Thine assistance,
Every plant should droop and die.

Surely once Thy garden flourish'd!
Every part look'd gay and green;
Then Thy Word our spirits nourish'd;
Happy seasons we have seen!
But a drought has since succeeded,
And a sad decline we see;
Lord, Thy help is greatly needed,
Help can only come from Thee!

Where are those we counted leaders,
Fill'd with zeal and love and truth—
Old professors, tall as cedars,
Bright examples of our youth?
Some, in whom we once delighted,
We shall meet no more below;
Some, alas! we fear are blighted,
Scarce a single leaf they show.

Younger plants—the sight how pleasant!
Cover'd thick with blossoms stood;
But they cause us grief at present,
Frosts have nipp'd them in the bud!
Dearest Saviour, hasten hither,
Thou canst make them bloom again;
Oh, permit them not to wither,
Let not all our hopes be vain!

Let our mutual love be fervent,
Make us prevalent in prayers;
Let each one esteem'd Thy servant
Shun the world's bewitching snares.
Break the tempter's fatal power,
Turn the stony heart to flesh;
And begin, from this good hour,
To revive Thy work afresh.

Conclusion

The aim of this book has been to spell out a heart-cry for revival in terms of biblical teaching in the context of contemporary need. All that remains is to illustrate what has been said with some stories of what will happen when we *believe* God to send revival. The examples I have chosen cover the areas of the personal life, the local church, and the mission field.

Perhaps the most vivid recollection I have of revival in a personal life is the story of Evan Roberts, the leader of the Welsh revival of 1904-5. When he died on January 29, 1951, in a little nursing home in Cardiff, at the age of seventy-two, the *News Chronicle* wrote that "Wales mourns her greatest prophet."

Evan Roberts was born at Loughor in 1878 and after a period as miner and blacksmith he entered the grammar school at Newcastle-Emlyn in preparation for the Christian ministry. Even in those days God was beginning to stir in his young heart, giving him an insatiable hunger for heaven-sent revival. Indeed, it was while he was at this school that he attended a conference at Blaenanerch, in September 1904, convened to consider the spiritual life of the churches in the area and to decide on what action to take. It was during the conference that Evan Roberts was "filled with the Holy Spirit."

For thirteen years, writes Evan Roberts, I had prayed for the Spirit; and this is the way I was led to pray. William Davies, the deacon, said one night in the society: "Remember to be faithful. What if the Spirit descended and you were absent? Remember Thomas! What a loss he had."

I said to myself: "I will have the Spirit"; and through every kind of weather and in spite of all difficulties, I went to the meetings. Many times, on seeing other boys with the boats on the tide, I was tempted to turn back and join them. But, no, I said to myself: "Remember your resolve," and on I went. I went faithfully to the meetings for prayer throughout the ten or eleven years I prayed for a Revival. It was the Spirit that moved me thus to think.

During a morning meeting which Evan Roberts attended, the evangelist pleaded that the Lord would "bend us." The Spirit seemed to say to Roberts, "That's what you need, to be bent." And thus he describes his experience:

I felt a living force coming into my bosom. This grew and grew, and I was almost bursting. My bosom was boiling. What boiled in me was that verse: "God commending His love." I fell on my knees with my arms over the seat in front of me; the tears and perspiration flowed freely. I thought blood was gushing forth.

Certain friends approached to wipe his face. Meanwhile he was crying out, "O Lord, bend me! Bend me!" Then suddenly the glory broke.

Mr. Roberts adds:

After I was bent, a wave of peace came over me, and the audience sang, "I hear Thy welcome voice." And as they sang I thought about the bending at the Judgment Day, and I was filled with compassion for those that would have to bend on that day, and I wept.

Henceforth, the salvation of souls became the burden of my heart. From that time I was on fire with a desire to go through all Wales, and if it were possible, I was willing to pray God for the privilege of going.

From that point onward, this young man of twenty-six went everywhere spreading the fires of revival. The chapels were thronged, with hundreds more outside. His appearance at these gatherings often caused much religious fervor and excitement, and a few words of exhortation or a brief prayer sufficed to set the congregation ablaze. The people would burst into singing and then testimony, followed by prayer, and then into singing again. Indeed, it is said that all Wales seemed like a praise meeting. Mealtimes and other routine practices were neglected and forgotten, and God moved throughout the whole principality in saving and purifying power. Heaven-sent revival had truly visited Wales.

The point of the story is that it all started with a man who was prepared to pray, "O Lord, bend me! Bend me!" Can this happen today? I most certainly believe it can.

What can happen in the area of the personal life can also take place in a local church. To back this up, I want to quote quite extensively from the story of the Reverend Joseph Kemp, as told by his wife.

Joseph Kemp was an orphan whom God gloriously saved in the 1880's, and prepared as a vessel unto honor, meet for the Master's use. After some training at the Bible Institute of Glasgow, Mr. Kemp was led into small pastorates and then finally to the now well-known Charlotte Chapel of

Edinburgh. After a most fruitful ministry in that city he came over to the United States to become the minister of Calvary Baptist Church, New York City. Subsequently, he went to New Zealand, where he led the work at the Auckland Baptist Tabernacle. During his closing years he founded the New Zealand Bible Institute and was greatly used in bringing blessing and revival to churches, as well as to individual lives, throughout the whole of that land.

My main concern, however, is what happened at Charlotte Chapel under his God-anointed ministry. And here let me refer directly to his biography:

Soon after the Welsh revival broke out, I went to Wales, where I spent two weeks watching, experiencing, drinking in, having my own heart searched, comparing my methods with those of the Holy Spirit; and then I returned to my people in Edinburgh to tell what I had seen. In Wales I saw the people had learned to sing in a way which to me was new. I never heard such singing as theirs. They sang such old familiar hymns as "When I survey the wondrous Cross," and "There is a fountain filled with Blood," and "I need Thee, oh, I need Thee." They needed no organist or choir or leader. Their singing was natural. The Holy Spirit was in their singing as much as in any other exercise. They had the New Song. People tell us our religion is joyless. Well, if the saints of the Living God have no joy, who has? Jesus Christ has given us to see that joy is one of the qualities He imparts to the saints of God. The world knows nothing of it. Do not tell me that the sporting clubs, the dance halls, the movies, and operas can give you joy. They can for the moment give you some fun, but that is not joy. Joy is the gift of God. When a revival from God visits a congregation it brings joy with it.

The dominating note of the Welsh revival was redemption through the Blood. There, too, was the recognition of the Lordship of Christ. It is the same old story from age to age. There is no new way of bringing men to Christ. There must be the recognition of sin, and the joyful recognition that sin can be blotted out by the Blood of the Lamb, and a Bloodwashed soul kept and sanctified by the Lord Jesus Christ.

The evening he returned from Wales was memorable. A large meeting was in full swing when he walked down the aisle of the chapel. The people listened eagerly as he told of his visit and its effect upon his own soul. After telling the story he tested the meeting, asking if there was a man willing to be saved. About five seats from the front a man rose, saying, "I want you to pray for me." This man was the first of hundreds who were saved during the revival in Charlotte Chapel.

The people were now on tiptoe with expectancy for a revival. A Conference on January 22, 1906, addressed by several workers who had visited Wales, lasted from 3:30 p.m. until midnight. From that day it was felt that the fire of God had fallen; and as far as Charlotte Chapel was concerned, God had answered prayer and reviving had come. By the end of 1905, the church had been praying one whole year without a break. Night after night, week after week, month after month, the prayer meetings went on increasing in numbers and intensity. It is impossible to convey any adequate idea of the prayer passion that characterized those meetings. There was little or no preaching, it being a common experience for the pastor to go to the pulpit on the Lord's Day, and find the congregation so caught in the spirit of prayer as to render preaching out of the question.

The people poured out their hearts in importunate prayer. I have yet to witness a movement that has produced more permanent results in the lives of men, women and children. There were irregularities, no doubt; some commotion, yes. The momentum and power of God's Spirit shattered all conventionality. But such a dynamic movement is to be preferred far above the dull, dreary, monotonous decorum of many church-es. Under these influences the crowds thronged the chapel, which only three years before maintained a "sombre vacuum." After the first year of this work no fewer than one thousand souls had been personally dealt with, who had been brought to God during the prayer meetings.

"It is impossible to record in detail the striking inci-dents of the revival movement in 1905," Mr. Kemp wrote. "If its genuineness can be attested by its results, then we need have no doubt regarding it. It has given us a full church night and morning, which of itself is some-thing to be profoundly thankful for in days when it is conceded the churches have lost their hold on the people. It has given us a most loyal and devoted band of workers, whose aim is the glory of God in the salvation of sinners. It has taught us to pray in a fashion few of us knew of be-fore. It has given to both young and old a new love for the Bible. Time would fail to tell of the purified lives, changed homes, and the brightened outlook of hun-dreds.

"In 1906 the movement seemed to have found its level, and arrangements were made to reorganize the work on generally accepted church lines. But again the revival fires blazed forth, and the meetings became marked by a deeper outgoing of the soul to God in prayer than ever; and a passionately expressed desire for the salvation of men was a dominant feature. Towards the close of 1906 there were indications that the Lord was about to move in our midst once more. The attendances at the 7 a.m. prayer meetings on Lord's Days increased, and the meet-ings were marked by a deepening spirit of prayer. This was followed up by the same prayer spirit in the week-night meetings.

"On Saturday, December 20, our monthly conference and evening meetings were addressed by friends who had previously experienced a quickening in their own souls: and their testimony, given in the power of the Holy Ghost, awakened longings in the hearts of many for Revival. One and another, some secretly, some publicly, claimed Divine anointing for service. Some went home that Saturday night, but could not sleep. One brother told the next day how the deep conviction that the Revival so long prayed for was at hand, had kept him awake for the most part of the night. A singular and remarkable thing is, that many who were not present at these meetings had at the same time the impression borne in on them that the Lord was about to work.

"The meetings on Lord's Day were marked by an earnest outgoing of the soul to God in prayer, and a passionately expressed desire for the salvation of men, all of which told of the dealings many had had—Jacob-like—with God alone. It was, however, at a late prayer meeting, held in the evening at 9:30, that the fire of God fell. There was nothing, humanly speaking, to account for what happened. Quite suddenly, upon one and another came an overwhelming sense of the reality and awfulness of His presence and of eternal things. Life, death, and eternity seemed suddenly laid bare. Prayer and weeping began, and gained in intensity every moment. As on the day of laying the foundation of the second temple, 'the people could not discern the noise of the shout of joy from the noise of the weeping of the people' (Ezra 3:13). One was overwhelmed before the sudden bursting of the bounds. Could it be real? We looked up and asked for clear directions, and all we knew of guidance was, 'Do nothing.' Friends who were gathered sang on their knees. Each seemed to sing, and each seemed to pray, oblivious of one another.

"Then the prayer broke out again, waves and waves of prayer; and the midnight hour was reached. The hours had passed like minutes. It is useless being a spectator looking on, or praying for it, in order to catch its spirit and breath. It is necessary to be in it, praying in it, part of it, caught by the same power, swept by the same wind. One who was present says: 'I cannot tell you what Christ was to me last night. My heart was full to overflowing. If ever my Lord was near to me, it was last night.'

"Our programme drawn up for the watchnight service and New Year's Day had to give way before this Divine visitation. Early on the last night of the old year, friends gathered for prayer, and continued until the beginning of the watchnight service at 10:30, at which meeting the power of the Lord was again manifest. What the closing hours of 1906 meant to many only the Eternal Day will reveal. Crushed, broken, and penitent on account of the defeated past, many of us again knelt at the Cross; and as the bells rang in the New Year, we vowed by God's grace to press into our lives more service for Him, to be more like Him in spirit and walk, and win to Him our fellow-men.

"The Chapel was opened all day on the 1st of January, and meetings were held at 11, 3 and 6:30. At every meeting, especially in the afternoon and evening, God drew near. The afternoon meeting got entirely beyond a cut-and-dried programme, and resolved itself into one of prayer, confession, testimony, and praise. Testimonies from friends at home and visitors from a distance were given to the fresh power which had come into their lives. The evening meeting went on without the guidance of any human hand; and though friends were present who had been engaged to address it, no address could be given. The people were bowed in prayer, heart-searching, and contrition. And it was only while thus waiting that light broke in upon many hearts, once more revealing and bringing to light the 'hidden things of darkness' and compelling separation from sin unto God. During the meetings a number of unconverted persons decided for Christ; but the burden of all the meetings was that 'judgment must begin at the house of God.'

"Meetings of a similar character have been going on

for over a fortnight. To the curious, the meetings appear disorderly; but to those who are in them and of them, there is order in the midst of disorder. The confusion never gets confused; the meetings are held by invisible Hands. Believers have been awakened to a sense of having lived defeated lives, bound by the 'law of sin and death'; progress retarded by 'weights' and 'sins'; spiritual growth stunted by habits of various kinds. Over all these things victory has been claimed. Brethren have been reconciled to one another; differences which kept sisters apart have been destroyed. Many have testified to victory over novel-reading, dancing, theatre-going, etc. Beyond our ordinary services on Lord's Day, there has been very little or no preaching. While the work has been chiefly confined to the saints of God, purifying, humbling, purging, cleansing, there have been numerous conversions. But these have all taken place during the time of prayer, and prayer usually of a tumultous sort. One does not readily take in the meaning of simultaneous praying, in a meeting of from 100 to 200 people, full to overflowing of a strong desire to pour out their hearts before the Lord. How could there possibly be time for each to pray separately? After all, what need is there to wait? His ear finds no difficulty in dealing with the simultaneous prayer of a revival meeting.

"We ought not to be disturbed by such happenings. If we could permit ourselves to forget our neighbours and everything else, and remember that we are in the presence of God, we should very soon pass the place where such things could disturb. We appeal for a freedom of the Holy Spirit on our gatherings, and, as one eminent writer has said: 'God save us, lest we civilise the Holy Spirit out of our churches.'

"What the present movement is doing is the creating of a new intensity of love to Jesus, a new sensitiveness to sin, a new desire to have victory in the inner life, a new passion in prayer, and a new expectancy to see God work in power. To all who know anything of the inner spirit of the recent movement, the conviction is given: 'He hath shed forth this which we now see and hear' (Acts 2:33). This awakening and quickening was so spontaneous and almost unlooked for that we are compelled to aknowledge its Divine origin. It has not passed off and vanished in mere sentiment; nor like a wave of emotion proved itself transient and unreal. It abides. At the moment of writing, it shows no sign of abatement, but rather have we evidence of its deepening and expanding nature. Many who, in the earlier stages of its manifestation, looked coldly, and critically, and suspiciously upon it, have been brought into line with it. For nigh thirty days the Spirit of God has been brooding over us. Come, O Breath, and breathe in this manner upon us now. Amen, O Lord."

A second half-night of prayer was held on January 13, but the spirit and scenes of that meeting baffle description. It was given to some of us to know what Isaiah meant when he cried, "The posts of the door moved at the voice of Him that cried."

Some of the choruses of the revival movement were:

> *He can break every fetter,*
> *He can set you free.*

—with variations of "Let Him break every fetter," and "He has broken every fetter"—

> *Victory for me! through the blood of Christ my Saviour,*
> *Victory for me! through the precious Blood.*

and

> *Sinful and black though the past may have been;*
> *Many the crushing defeats I have seen,*
> *Yet on Thy promise, O Lord, now I lean,*
> *Cleansing for me.*

The singing of these choruses was the means of bringing many souls from bondage to liberty.

On February 16, 1907, Mr. Kemp wrote: "Among the many remarkable features of the recent spiritual awakening in our midst, none has been more striking than the all-night prayer meeting held on February 16. Beginning at ten o'clock on the Saturday night, it continued until eight o'clock on Lord's Day morning. The only break during the whole night was at two o'clock, when tea was served. Fully two hundred people would be present until that hour, and not fewer than one hundred and fifty remained the whole of the night.

"It is not possible to describe such a meeting; it is necessary to be in it to know it. From the beginning to the close the prayers ascended in one unbroken continuity. At times the prayers rose and fell like the waves of the sea. At half-past three in the morning the scenes were bewildering to behold. It seemed as though everybody in the meeting was praying at once. There was no confusion: nothing unseemly. The passion of prayer had caught the people, and we felt we must pray.

"The Lord's Day following, over a score of souls professed faith in Christ, again proving the faithfulness of our God. Space forbids us entering into details on this remarkable season of prayer.

"Prayer meetings have been continued nightly, and we look for some brothers and sisters to receive an abiding blessing, which in the days to come will mark them out in a very special way for effective service."

On March 1907 he again writes: "The gracious visitation, reported at some length last month, has deepened as the weeks have gone past. The marked features of the movement are—

"1. A deep conviction of sin, even where the outward life appeared blameless. Nothing has been so remarkable as the searching of heart and the revealing of the 'hidden things.' Many things thought to be right have been seen to be wrong and sinful.

"At one never-to-be-forgotten prayer meeting, as we were approaching midnight, a request for prayer was made by one, that grace might be granted to give up an unconverted sweetheart. No fewer than four similar cases were the subjects of prayer that night, and in each case these unholy attachments were dropped. To very many, 'sin does not appear sin'; but in few things does sin hide its true colors more effectively than in the matter of the 'unequal yoke.' For a child of God, be they man or woman, to allow the affections to be placed upon one who is unconverted, is to commit no light offence against the plain teaching of the Word of God, and must bring with it a whole horde of sorrows. Thank God, many during these weeks of quickening have had shown to them the sinfulness of that line of action, and grace has been given to forsake the evil way.

"Others have been convicted of prayerlessness, indolence, worldliness, temper, bitterness, and so on. Here the 'Doctrine of the doubtful things' applies. A thing which may have been in itself perfectly lawful, has been abandoned because it stood in the way of full surrender and wholehearted consecration.

"2. Another feature is the prolonged intercession sometimes for hours. Our usual seven o'clock prayer meeting, held every Lord's Day morning, has for several weeks commenced at six o'clock and continued until eight o'clock. The 5:45 p.m. prayer meeting starts at 5:30, and such has been the power of God in the meetings that it has been impossible to get to the open air at the usual hour, the Upper Vestry and the Pastor's Vestry and the Library all crowded with praying people. Then again at 9:30 p.m., after the Lord's Day work is over, about sixty have met again for prayer, and continued until after midnight. Here we have learned something of what Wales experienced of prolonged prayer meetings.

"Not only have lengthened meetings been a feature of the work, but the gift of prolonged intercession has been given to several brethren. Losing all consciousness of another's presence, the soul has poured itself out, often audibly, for over an hour. One brother, unknown to any of us, prayed in an agony for the people of his own town for fully an hour and a half. The perspiration was standing on his brow like beads. He was almost too weak to stand when the hour came for closing the chapel, and was literally lifted from his position.

"3. The third marked feature is the new spontaneity and power of the Prayer Meetings. There is no necessity to ask anyone to 'improve the time.' The stream of prayer flows on unhindered. Many who never prayed in public before have found it easy to speak to God in the presence of others. To be in such prayer meetings is the privilege of a lifetime. Before this movement, such meetings were known only by name. They had been features in past revivals, but unknown to the most of us in this day; now they are part of our Christian experience. Prayer at such meetings is not a mere perfunctory exercise, cold and meaningless, but a living vital reality."

Summing up this remarkable revival, Dr. A. C. Dixon, who knew Kemp and his ministry quite intimately, gave this evaluation: "I consider that Mr. Kemp's work in Charlotte Chapel, Edinburgh, to be more lasting and further reaching than the Welsh revival." It may be that some pastor is reading this little book. You ask the question: Could such a thing ever happen in my church? Once again, the answer is that I am sure it could. Do we not believe that "Jesus Christ [is] the same yesterday, and today, and for ever" (Hebrews 13:8)?

Now concerning the mission field. It is generally acknowledged that the East African revival is the longest and most remarkable of any spiritual awakening on that continent, or anywhere else in the world. One of the best-known products of that spiritual movement is Bishop Festo Kivengere. In an interview with the editors of *Christianity Today*, the Bishop answered a number of questions which help us to understand what a heaven-sent revival can mean on the mission field.

Question. What is the East African revival, and why has it lasted over forty years?

Answer. Can I explain? This is a question I have been asked repeatedly for over twenty-five years, and all I have ever been able to do is to share what I have seen. The only explanation I can give is that it is God's work. It is not a technique. It is a movement that cannot be contained. It is renewal within renewal. It is an attitude toward the Lord, toward the Bible, toward the fellowship, and toward the Spirit. It has always been open to a fresh touch.

Q. What does this revival mean to the people involved in it?

A. It is when Christ becomes a living, risen Lord in the life of a believer. For the non-believer, it is when he is brought into a confrontation with Christ and accepts him as Savior, thus completely changing his life morally and socially. In other words, revival is when Christ becomes alive in a life, changing that life. The person is born again, and if he has previously had that experience, then his life is changed in such a way that it affects all his relationships.

Q. Is it visible to an outsider?

A. Absolutely! Go back to a village a week after a man comes to the Lord in a meeting in the market. The whole village knows something about it. He has paid the debts he owes. He has gone to people he hated and said, "I'm sorry. I'm a changed man." He has apologized or asked for forgiveness. He's now telling them what Christ means to him. He has carried his new belief into his business practices. In other words, it isn't something he sits on as a comfortable experience. If anything, it is terribly uncomfortable.

Q. How has this differed from other revivals in history?

A. It may be the continued willingness of those who have been revived to be renewed by the Spirit of God. At the Kabale convention celebrating the fortieth year of the revival in that area, we heard up-to-date testimonies from people who were brought to Christ as early as 1930. They had tremendous freshness; yet they had been winning souls for thirty-five or forty years. They have remained open to what the Spirit may want to say to them in the present situation. They learned that when they got into a rut God had to turn them out of it so they could breathe again. The tendency to get into certain patterns can stifle the work of the Spirit and create pockets of hardness. Continued breaking and bringing new streams of life have been the means God has used.

Q. Amid this openness are there some agreed points of emphasis?

A. Yes, three. The basis was the Bible. Christ was at the center. And the Word was not just read; it was obeyed.

Q. How has the Bible been used?

A. It has been preached from Genesis to Revelation. Men who have never been to seminary have taught it as the living book. I know people who were converted at the age of forty-five, born again when they were illiterate. They taught themselves how to read immediately. Even before they could read they quoted what had been quoted to them. They would get the verses in their heads and then go stand up and preach them without having a Bible. They preached it without hesitation, and they allowed it to work on them. They have won hundreds and thousands of people, and I believe their power lay in their attitude of feeding on the Word. Of course, they have no commentaries, so as you can imagine they are limited. But the amazing thing is that they can see the whole spectrum of the Bible in such a way that one must agree they are in fellowship with the Author, the Holy Spirit. To them it is God's Word. It speaks to them, and they do something about it. It convicts them, and they repent. It fills their hearts with joy.

Q. Explain, please, the centrality of Christ in the revival.

A. All sorts of things have happened: dreams, visions in the night, conviction of sin; but no one ever put these above Christ and him crucified and moving alive among us. We had our excesses, but they were corrected as we kept our eyes on the Word incarnate and preached the written Word.

Q. What about the third point you mentioned, obedience to the Word?

A. The living Christ in the Bible spoke living words to living persons in living situations. This meant that those who listened had to do something about it. It made men move. It made them pay debts of love and money. It made people go back and speak to neighbors out of compelling love and concern for their souls. The Word compelled men and women to evangelize.

Q. Has this evangelizastion spilled across tribal and national boundaries?

A. Oh, yes. It has gone into all parts of Uganda, Ruanda, Burundi, Kenya, Tanzania, and Malawi, and into parts of Ethiopia. And it has had an impact in such faraway places as Indonesia.

Q. Is it interdenominational?

A. Initially, the thrust was in the Church of England, but the fire began to move, and people shared with those in other denominations. It went from church to church, denomination to denomination. Some churches, like the Lutherans, found it hard to move fast at first. They were looking at it from a doctrinal point of view. The very staunch evangelical groups found it terribly hard to accept at first look. Doctrinal loopholes could be found. It didn't have a neat theological approach. They felt that things might go wild. Imagine 300 people lying on the ground weeping and crying and shouting and shrieking in church. Invite *that* sort of thing into your church?

Q. They were afraid of enthusiasm?

A. Exactly! Those who saw this considered it too risky. They did not know how to control it.

Q. Were the top leaders of the Anglican church involved from the beginning?

A. No. That would be great for Anglicans if God blessed the men with commanding positions and influence. But he came and blessed girls and elderly women and boys and nobodies, and the ministers remained very dry. Of course, the ministers were embarrassed by what these lively Christians said, and they opposed the revival. Until the pastor was blessed, he had to oppose it. Why did God choose to work "through the back door"? Why not deal with the big man so things could move easily?

Q. How did the "big men" get involved?

A. One example was in Tanzania where some of us went to witness. The doors were shut against us repeatedly. The African pastor got up in the cathedral pulpit one Sunday when the church was packed and said, "Now, look: I want to warn you against some strangers who have recently moved in. They talk big words about salvation, but they are wolves in sheep's skin. Be careful of them." And you could see the congregation turn and look at us. Sunday after Sunday this man did not preach anything. Finally, he got up one morning and said, "This is my last warning. If any of you is caught up in this talk and business of salvation I will excommunicate you for six months to show you how wrong you are." There was silence. We walked outside. We were becoming bitter.

Then the Lord spoke to me and said, "You owe deep love to that man. You need to be helpful. Go to his church, and do what you can, and love him." We protested that it would be difficult, but we went on for a few weeks, for a month, for three months, for five months. Finally he stood before his congregation one day with tears streaming down his cheeks. He said to them, "Months ago I told you that if any of you experienced this salvation they were talking about I would excommunicate you. I have been saved. Now you can excommunicate me if you like." We could hardly believe our ears.

Public testimony! This man was born again because revival started. But it didn't start easily.

Q. Why has this been accepted by leaders of the mainline denominations in East Africa, such as the Anglican, when it might not have been accepted elsewhere?

A. It was not accepted at first. That is a part of the picture that has not been reported widely. In Uganda, for instance, twenty students who had only two months or less to go before ordination were expelled from our theological college. They were expelled simply because the warden was not agreeable to their experience, and the bishop agreed with him. I got a lovely letter about a year ago from that bishop, who is now retired in England. He has been deeply blessed in the years since that. We went to see him when we conducted a mission in England. It was interesting that before revival broke out in the country he had asked for missions of evangelistic teams to spread throughout Uganda. He was the only bishop there then, and he had a vision, but many of his ministers were not born again. Then God began to move, and people were repenting of their sins. People were in tears. A respectable part of the church was embarrassed. Ministers did not like it. This poor man, the bishop, was afraid, and he shied away from what he had actually initiated. He turned around and said, "This can't be of God; it must be of the Devil." So for twenty-five years he opposed it, but the position of the hierarchy didn't stop the movement.

I was brought into it when things in the church were really thick and hard, when licenses were being withdrawn from ministers and the revival groups were not permitted to meet in churches. But God did something unique. After the bishop himself suggested that we leave and form another denomination, we went and had prayer. The Spirit of God said, "Don't you move." So, our answer was, "This is our church here, and we stay whether we speak or not." We witnessed, people suffered every week, and one minister after another came into the blessing of God. Now more than 85 percent of the clergymen know Jesus Christ as their Saviour, as do all our bishops.

Q. To what extent has the charismatic emphasis been a part of the East African revival?

A. None. There are now some charismatic groups in Africa, but they seem to have come through European and American missionaries. In one country I visited, a man told me, "We *had* a revival." When I asked him when, he replied that it had been three years earlier. Then I asked him exactly what he meant by "*had* a revival." His response was that it was the extraordinary experiences, the unusual manifestations, and now that they were over, so was the "revival." But real revival is Jesus Christ himself. Now, I do not despise the manifestations God has sent to shake people up. Praise God for them! I have told people who have been involved: "Don't think the manifestations are going to feed you. They shook you up so that you may go to the bread of life." Perhaps the only contribution I have made to some of these groups is that I have reminded them not to overlook the fundamental issues.

Q. Is there anything distinctively African in the East African revival that cannot be found in other cultures or that cannot be used in other countries?

A. That is difficult to say. Maybe our music or other forms of expression have made a certain contribution. But when we have gone to share it in the South Pacific or in Central America and elsewhere, we have shared Christ and not Africa. In Indonesia and other places God has done some wonderful things. No, I don't think there is anything purely African about the revival.

What a difference it would make on the mission fields of the world if the overseas churches were to be visited by a similar outpouring of the Holy Spirit! Surely it is time for missionary statesmen, as well as pastors of churches in the homeland, to give more attention to the crying need for prayer, faith and revival. Whether it be in the personal life, in the church life, or on the mission field, we need revival, we need revival urgently, we need revival desperately. Oh, that our heart-cry might be:

> *Let it come, O Lord, we pray Thee,*
> *Let the show'r of blessing fall;*
> *We are waiting, [and expecting],*
> *Oh, revive the hearts of all.*
> *James L. Black*